T0357256

MAKE YOUR MARK

MAKE YOUR MARK

LESSONS IN CHARACTER FROM SEVEN PRESIDENTS

MARK K. UPDEGROVE

HARPER

An Imprint of HarperCollinsPublishers

HarperCollins books may be purchased for educational, business, or sales promotional use. For information, please email the Special Markets Department at SPsales@harpercollins.com.

FIRST EDITION

Library of Congress Cataloging-in-Publication Data has been applied for.

ISBN 978-0-06-343016-7

25 26 27 28 29 LBC 5 4 3 2 1

To

Isabel and Maggie,
Charlie,
Mateo and Maddie,
and
Tallie

CONTENTS

MAKE YOUR MARK

INTRODUCTION

Clare Boothe Luce, the trailblazing congresswoman from Connecticut and Pulitzer Prize–winning playwright of *The Women*, used to lecture the presidents she knew—from Herbert Hoover to Ronald Reagan.

"A great man is one sentence," she said. "History has no time for more than one sentence, and it is always a sentence that has an active verb."

She would then illustrate. Lincoln: "He preserved the union and freed the slaves." Franklin Roosevelt: "He lifted us out of the Great Depression and helped us win a world war."

Finally, she would challenge them: "What is *your* sentence?"

When she posed the question to John F. Kennedy just weeks before the Cuban Missile Crisis, he dismissed it by informing her, "I am not interested in my place in history."

Nonsense. Kennedy aimed to be a great president and had an eye on history, which he read passionately. He also knew she was right; while not confined to one sentence, history is often drawn in the most succinct of terms. If it regards a president at all, it is bound to be a concise assessment of his most consequential and far-reaching deeds, whether they reflect on him positively or not.

But underlying history's judgment, cursory or otherwise, are defining character traits that infuse his legacy.

After Richard Nixon triumphantly visited China in 1972, paving the road toward normalized diplomatic relations and changing the dynamic in the Cold War, Luce suggested Nixon's sentence might be, "He went to China."

After he resigned due to the unraveling Watergate scandal, Nixon suspected that the sentence was more likely to be, "He resigned the office."

In truth, it's probably both, revealing the best and worst of Nixon's complex character, that of a bold foreign policy visionary who sought to improve America's position in the world and a paranoid politician who broke the law to better ensure the retention of presidential power.

Nixon's historical fate is a reminder that in leadership, character matters above all. This rings as true today as when the Greek philosopher Heraclitus wrote, "Character is destiny," nearly three thousand years ago.

It's especially true in the presidency, guiding our presidents through the weightiest hours in an office Franklin Delano Roosevelt called "preeminently a place of moral leadership." Luce's sentence for him—"He lifted us out of the Great Depression and helped us win a world war"— spoke to FDR's buoyancy in leading us through the biggest economic calamity in American history and his resolve to keep the world safe for democracy by prevailing in World War II.

Her sentence for Lincoln—"He preserved the union and freed the slaves"—attested to his will in keeping our nation whole by winning the Civil War and his compassion in seeing to the abolition of slavery.

Chance and circumstance invariably play a hand in the challenges a president must address, limiting the extent to which he can dictate the sentence he aspires to. FDR, for instance, knew that he would have to grapple with the Great Depression, which was ravaging the country when he took office, but he could not have foreseen World War II, which pulled in America inescapably after the Japanese bombed Pearl Harbor. Regardless, character is the rudder that directs his deeds and decisions, and, in large measure, our nation's course.

Throughout my career as an author, publisher, journalist, television commentator, and head of a presidential library and foundation, I have had the privilege of interviewing and hosting seven US presidents. My access to and study of those men has given me a firm sense of their character and how it came to bear in their legacies, while informing my own leadership journey. In these pages I'll offer sketches of every president from Gerald Ford through Barack Obama, reflecting on the character trait that underlies his most significant accomplishments:

Ford's instinct to do the right thing in the wake of Watergate;

Jimmy Carter's mission to do good in the areas of peace and human rights during his presidency and throughout his postpresidency;

Ronald Reagan's optimism, changing the dynamic of the Cold War and restoring the nation's confidence and pride after a sustained period of demoralizing setbacks;

George H. W. Bush's humility, helping to ensure a peaceful end to the Cold War, which had seethed between the superpowers for over forty years;

Bill Clinton's resilience and determination to keep working for the American people in the face of political and personal obstacles;

George W. Bush's lifesaving charge to give back as the AIDS epidemic spread unchecked throughout much of the developing world;

and Barack Obama's grace as the first African American to hold the country's highest office.

It is not my intention to aggrandize these men or to suggest that all will be seen as great leaders who have earned a place in the presidential pantheon. Each had his own trials, and none succeeded as he may have wished.

Ford, the first and only president to be unelected on a national ballot, was unable to win the presidency in his own right. Carter and George H. W. Bush were defeated for reelection as their public support eroded. Reagan was embroiled in the Iran-Contra affair, while Clinton became the first president to be impeached in 130 years owing to his sexual involvement with a White House intern. George W. Bush initiated failed wars in Iraq and Afghanistan; Obama was unable to keep the electorate from a swing toward nativism and populism.

Each will earn a different grade for his turn in the White House. But, in my view, each loved our country, put its interests above his own, and did his best. We can ask for little more.

Collectively, these portraits will illustrate that there is no one-size-fits-all model for leadership. Each president had a unique set of strengths and weaknesses, just as we all do. In many respects, they are a mirror of us as a people, reflecting our talents, flaws, virtues, frailties, struggles, and ambitions. At their best, they made their marks by reflecting the values we aspire to as a nation—and we can learn from them.

By challenging ourselves to never lose sight of the importance of character and striving to find the best in ourselves, we can make our own marks as leaders. As you read about these presidents, I hope you'll ask yourself, How does my leadership reflect my character? How do I want to be seen? What do I want to achieve? How will I make *my* mark?

GERALD R. FORD / DOING WHAT'S RIGHT

The decision weighed heavily on the mind of Jerry Ford. The University of Michigan Wolverines' star center, linebacker, and soon-to-be "Most Valuable Player," Ford was in his senior year and in the midst of the losing 1934 season when he was jarred by a crisis of conscience. It involved his friend and roommate, Willis Ward, the only Black member of the team. Ward had joined the Wolverines the previous year, a walk-on who earned a spot as right end and would become the runner-up for the Associated Press's Big Ten Athlete of the Year Award. But Ward's athletic prowess mattered less to their opponents in the third game of the season, the Georgia State Yellow Jackets, than the color of his skin. The team refused to play the Wolverines if Ward took the field. In the face of controversy, Michigan's athletic director yielded to Georgia State's Jim Crow demand.

Ford wrestled with whether he should quit the team in protest. His stepfather advised him otherwise. So did Ward, who urged him to play for the sake of the team, which had lost its first two games of the season after winning national championships the two previous years. Wouldn't beating the Yellow Jackets be the most powerful statement the Wolverines could make? Ford decided Ward was right. The following Saturday, he dutifully donned his number 48 jersey and aided the team toward a 29–2 victory, their only win of the eight-game season.

During play, after a Yellow Jacket linebacker taunted, "Where's your n****r player?" Ford and a teammate answered with a punishing clean hit that sent him reeling to the ground, where he was scooped up and carried off the field on a stretcher. "That was for you," Ford told Ward later.

* * *

Jerry Ford could always be counted on to do the right thing. It was how he was raised, reared by strong midwestern parents to be honest, hardworking, and mindful of the greater good.

Born Leslie King Jr. on June 14, 1913, Ford was the product of a broken marriage. Just weeks after his birth, his mother, Dorothy, fled a physically abusive husband in Omaha, Nebraska, for her hometown of Grand Rapids, Michigan, where she met and married Gerald R. Ford Sr., a paint salesman, who would give her toddler son his name and raise him as his own. "Junie," as he was called in his early years, later "Jerry," grew up as though he had sprung from the pages of the Horatio Alger novels his stepfather gave him in his youth, propelled by a healthy middle-class work ethic and a bent toward self-improvement. Growing to a strapping six feet, he endeavored to control a quick temper while achieving high school distinction as a member of the National Honor Society, a varsity athlete in basketball, track, and football, and an Eagle Scout, making him the only president to achieve Scouting's highest designation.

He went on to the University of Michigan during the depths of the Depression, frugally paying living expenses through a series of odd jobs and by regularly selling his blood to the university hospital for twenty-five dollars a pint. When he graduated, with a degree in economics, his senior yearbooks stated, "we can't really find anything nasty to say about him." Declining offers to play for the Green Bay Packers and Detroit Lions, he went east to Yale Law School, paying his way through as a coach for the football and boxing teams and graduating in the top third of his class. Afterward, he returned to Grand Rapids to practice law before being pulled into World War II, where, after requesting duty in a combat zone, he served as lieutenant commander on board the USS *Monterey*, earning nine combat medals during his service.

Back in Grand Rapids after the war, Ford soon felt the tug of politics. In 1948, at age thirty-five, he set his sights on the US House of Representatives, winning a steep uphill battle against a five-term incumbent congressman to capture the Republican nomination in Michigan's heavily Republican Fifth District, then coasting to victory in the November election.

A few weeks before the election, Ford married Betty

Bloomer, whom he had met the previous year. Strong and independent-minded, Betty had just moved back to her hometown of Grand Rapids from New York, where she danced for the company of Martha Graham while working as a fashion model to make ends meet. She was in the process of an amicable divorce and wanting nothing to do with men when she met Ford, an apparent exception. Just weeks after their wedding, the newlyweds packed their bags for a life in Washington that would last twenty-eight years, raising four children—three boys and one girl—along the way.

* * *

The first one to shake Ford's hand after he was sworn in on the House floor on the third day of January 1949 was a one-term Republican congressman of the same age. "I'm Dick Nixon from California," he said. "I welcome you here to the House chamber." It was no surprise that Nixon would seek out Ford; the two had a lot in common. Both were strivers from working-class backgrounds who had attended elite law schools, served as naval officers in the Pacific in World War II, won House seats from veteran incumbents against long odds, and arrived in Washington, DC, as young men to watch.

But there were differences too. Ford had earned his seat

through a shoe-leather effort in which he outcampaigned his competitor, stressing his position as a "converted internationalist" versus his isolationist opponent, as the Cold War against the Soviet Union became the dominant geopolitical issue. Nixon's victory in 1946 came by falsely accusing his opponent of having the endorsement of a political action committee that was alleged to have communist ties.

There was also the difference in their dispositions. Ford was easygoing, comfortable in his own skin. Despite his sharp mind, Nixon was dogged by insecurity and saddled with a chip on his shoulder. Then there was the difference in their ambitions: Ford aimed to be the Speaker of the House; Nixon aspired to the presidency.

Ford could little have realized that his political fate would ultimately be bound to the fellow congressman who had cordially extended his hand. Nor could he have known that they would be brought together in the White House a quarter of a century later as scandal pervaded the nation, rocking Americans' confidence in the institution of the presidency. In those dark days that would come later, it was the difference in character between the two men that really mattered.

Nixon, of course, would go on to fulfill his ambition—rising to become a senator, vice president to Dwight Eisenhower, and, after losing a close presidential election to John F. Kennedy, followed by a failed bid to the California governorship, winning the presidency in 1968 in a tight race against Hubert Humphrey, the incumbent vice president.

As Nixon rode the ups and downs of victory and defeat, Ford plodded along in the House, earning a reputation as "a congressman's congressman." Mostly though, Ford was seen by his colleagues in Congress as a nice guy—trustworthy, honest, decent. As the *New York Post* wrote of him shortly after his rise to minority leader, "He puts one in mind of a big sloppy dog capable of diving through the ice to rescue a drowning child."

Ford and Nixon remained in close contact through the years as leaders in the party. The two had a largely superficial relationship initially, and the admiration wasn't entirely mutual. Though Ford held out hope that Nixon would tap him as his running mate in 1960, openly campaigning for the position on the ticket, the call never came. In 1968, Nixon placed him on a short list of those he was considering as his number two, though largely as a courtesy to Ford. Instead, to the shock of many including Ford, he chose Spiro Agnew, the governor of Maryland, who had a reputation for law and order and would appeal to white southerners key to Nixon's election strategy.

Agnew remained on the ticket in 1972, as Nixon rode to the biggest presidential victory in history to that point. Then came Watergate.

The Watergate scandal started off with what would later

be called "a third rate burglary attempt" at the Democratic National Committee's headquarters in Washington's Watergate office complex in June 1972. Over time the scandal would unravel noxiously, revealing ties to others in the White House and eventually to Nixon himself, while showing a pattern of dirty tricks and deceit from the Nixon administration.

In late 1973, as the revelations of Watergate continued to swirl around Nixon, another scandal broke when Agnew was implicated for accepting kickbacks from state contractors during his tenure as Maryland governor. Agnew stepped down in the face of the charges, becoming the first vice president in history to resign the office.

It fell to an embattled Nixon to appoint his successor. Weakened by scandal and needing the confirmation of his appointee, Nixon nominated Ford—but reluctantly. Pointing to the chair behind the Resolute Desk, he asked an Oval Office visitor derisively, "Can you imagine Jerry Ford in this chair?"

Ford was quickly confirmed by Congress and sworn into the vice presidency in November 1973. Guileless and trusting, Ford took Nixon at face value when he said that he wasn't involved in the Watergate scandal, staunchly defending him in his new role. "My whole conduct as vice president was predicated on that personal trust," he said.

On August 5, 1974, Nixon's house of cards fell in. A

White House taping system captured a "smoking gun" conversation clearly showing he had participated in the cover-up of the Watergate burglary. Nixon had lied to Ford and to the rest of the country. For Ford, "the hurt was deep." The following day, he told Nixon he could no longer support him. So had congressional Republican leaders, who advised him that he would likely be impeached in the House and expelled by the Senate.

On August 8, Nixon announced that he would resign the presidency. By early the following morning, August 9, he was gone, boarding Marine One on the South Lawn, which took him on the first leg of a trip into exile at his home in San Clemente, California.

The burden of the office now fell to Ford, the first president to be unelected on a national ballot, and along with it the task of restoring the ebbing faith of Americans in their government. "We can do it," he whispered in Betty's ear as they repaired to the White House as Nixon was whisked away.

At noon, Ford was sworn into office in the East Room. Afterward, he offered not an inaugural address, but "a little straight talk among friends," pledging that "openness" would be the "hallmark" of his administration. "I am acutely aware that you have not elected me by your ballots, so I ask you to confirm me as your president with your prayers," he said, going on to declare: "Our long national nightmare is over. Our Constitution works. Our great republic is a government of laws and not men. Here the people rule."

But while Nixon had left the presidency, his legal fate hovered over the White House. As Ford grappled with the country's problems, including a foundering economy marked by inflation and slow growth and the unpopular, lingering war in Vietnam, questions about what would become of Nixon stood front and center, dividing Americans and crowding out his ability to focus on the problems at hand.

When asked during his vice presidential confirmation hearing about the possibility of a presidential pardon, Ford replied, "I don't think the public would stand for it."

As he settled into his job, however, he began to feel differently. A pardon could be the best means of moving on and repairing the divisions created by Watergate. The country, Ford concluded, needed "recovery, not revenge."

Less than a month after taking office, he had made up his mind. Among others, he called his old friend, Democratic House majority leader Thomas P. "Tip" O'Neill Jr., to let him know he was going to issue the pardon. "It's going to cost you the [presidential] election [in 1976]," O'Neill warned. But that wasn't the issue for Ford, who said simply, "It feels right in my heart."

On Sunday, September 8, Ford affixed his left-handed signature to a "full, free and absolute pardon unto Richard Nixon." That evening he explained his decision to the nation. "My conscience tells me that it is my duty, not only to proclaim domestic tranquility but to use every means that I have to ensure it," he said solemnly. "I do believe that the buck stops here, that I cannot rely upon opinion polls to tell me what is right."

Tranquility is not what he got. Overnight his lofty approval rating of 71 percent plunged, with two out of every three Americans opposed to the pardon, a reaction that was "far more serious" than he anticipated.

Ford never looked back. Just over two weeks later, in an interest to further move the country forward, he granted conditional amnesty to the more than fifty thousand young Americans who had either deserted their posts in the Vietnam War or dodged the draft altogether.

Other challenges came in the ensuing months. In the spring of 1975, Americans watched the harrowing fall of Saigon, the last gasp of the failed Vietnam War.

At home, Ford tried to tame intractable double-digit inflation, which he signaled he was combating by sporting a WIN button—an acronym for "Whip Inflation Now"—on the wide lapels of his often loud seventies-style double-knit suits that news anchor Tom Brokaw later joked needed pardons of their own.

Ford also battled an emerging image as a dim-witted clod, a caricature he inadvertently played into with a few high-profile stumbles and errant shots while golfing, a frequent pastime. On NBC's newly launched *Saturday Night*

A month into his presidency, Gerald R. Ford signs a "full, free and absolute pardon unto Richard Nixon," White House, September 8, 1974.

David Hume Kennerly, Center for Creative Photography, University of Arizona

Live, Chevy Chase depicted him clumsily pratfalling as he mindlessly went about his duties as president. Ford was a good sport about it, even delivering the program's signature line, "Live from New York, it's *Saturday Night*" on one of its airings, but the image didn't help him politically.

Neither did a challenge for the Republican presidential nomination in 1976 from Ronald Reagan. Ford staved off Reagan, but barely. In the general election he found himself pitted against former Georgia governor Jimmy Carter, who hammered away at the ills of the "Nixon-Ford" administration.

On Election Day, Carter slid by Ford, winning the popular vote by just 3 percentage points, with 7 percent of the electorate claiming they voted for Carter due solely to the pardon.

But Carter also saw the pardon's necessity. On January 20, 1977, he devoted the first lines of his Inaugural Address to Ford. "For myself and a grateful nation," he said, turning to the departing president, "I want to thank my predecessor for all he has done to heal our land."

* * *

In late 2004, Ford granted me what was to be one of his last interviews. We met on a bright fall morning at his California ranch-style home in Rancho Mirage. The ninety-one-year-old former president was a few minutes late. He had just fallen in his kitchen but insisted on keeping our appointment, arriving for our meeting a little wobbly and with a palpable lump on his head. "You're playing into a stereotype, Mr. President," I joked. Ford laughed gently. He was dressed comfortably in golf attire, confessing that his advanced age had reduced his golf rounds from nine holes, to six, to three.

Due to his diminishing hearing, we sat knee to knee behind the broad wooden desk in his spacious office. For a little more than an hour we discussed his life in and out of the White House. As we wound down, I asked him how he wanted to be remembered.

"That's easy, Mark," he replied. "I was a healer and a builder, and if I am to be remembered that way, I would be most grateful."

Jerry Ford got his wish. When he died the day after Christmas two years later after a long decline, he was heralded for modestly, courageously moving the country slowly forward out of the morass of Watergate and into a new day. In fact, he had seen in his nearly three decades out of the White House a marked reassessment of his fateful decision to pardon Nixon. Two-thirds of Americans stood against the pardon when it was granted, but by 1986, 54 percent believed it was the right decision.

After he was sworn into the vice presidency, Ford tempered expectations of his leadership by self-effacingly conceding that he was "a Ford, not a Lincoln," a sentiment that was embroidered on a pillow that would grace an armchair in his study after he moved on to the White House. Yet through his sheer decency and instinct to do right for the sake of the country, Ford elegantly fit his moment in history. There are times when we don't need greatness from our presidents. There are times when goodness will do.

JIMMY CARTER / DOING GOOD

Peace was nearly at hand. In September 1978, Jimmy Carter was close to doing what few thought possible, negotiating a settlement to the long-standing hostilities between Israel and Egypt.

For thirteen grueling days at Camp David, Carter scrupulously oversaw discussions between Israel's prime minister, Menachem Begin, and Egypt's president, Anwar Sadat, often acting as a go-between when they refused to talk to one another. Finally, it looked like they had reached an agreement and the prospect of a brighter day for the two Middle Eastern countries.

Then, at the last minute, Begin erupted in anger when he came across a concession Carter had made to Sadat, acknowledging that the Israeli capital of East Jerusalem, once part of Jordan, had been taken and occupied by Israel in the Six-Day War eleven years earlier. "We can pack our bags and go home without another word," Begin fumed before storming off to his cabin.

But Carter didn't let it go at that. Before Begin left the mountain retreat, he swallowed his own anger and made good on a promise to autograph photographs for Begin's eight grandchildren. Instead of signing each with "Best wishes, Jimmy Carter," as he would normally have done, his assistant tracked down the name of each child. Carter carefully inscribed them, writing their names followed by "Love and best wishes, Jimmy Carter." He hand-delivered the batch to Begin, who stiffly thanked him before looking down at the photos, reading the names of his grandchildren one by one—Michal, Orit, Meirav . . . Tears welled up in his eyes; Carter started to cry, too. "Let's try again," Begin said.

It was the turning point. The Camp David Accords became the framework for a historic treaty signed by Begin and Sadat on the White House lawn on a perfect spring day six months later. The result was a peace that has lasted ever since, a tribute to the courage of the two leaders and to Carter's stubborn will and fierce determination to overcome daunting odds to forge a better, healthier, more peaceful world. It was that same philanthropic ethos that had driven Carter throughout his life, a life that would improbably lead him to the White House with a campaign pledge to form a government "as good as the American people."

* * *

From his earliest days, Carter had a brimming confidence and the ability to do almost anything and do it well. So much so that his father, James Earl Carter Sr., a successful farmer and businessman, nicknamed him "Hotshot," or "Hot" for short. James Earl Carter Jr.—"Jimmy"—was born on October 1, 1924, in Plains, a hamlet in rural southwest Georgia, the first president to be born in a

Six months after negotiating the Camp David Accords, Jimmy Carter congratulates Anwar Sadat (left) and Menachem Begin after they signed a historic Egypt-Israel peace treaty, White House, March 26, 1979.

hospital. The oldest of four children, he grew up in Archery, two miles west of Plains, a product of churchgoing, field-working, segregated smalltown southern life. (Archery is now part of Plains.)

The Carters were the only white family among the fifty-some families that inhabited Archery. His mother, "Miss Lillian," a trained nurse who tended to both Black and white patients, openly rejected the racial prejudice that festered throughout the Deep South, making a last-ing impression on Jimmy. "All my playmates, all of my companions in the fields, the ones I hunted with, fished with, wrestled with, fought with, and loved, were Black people," Carter explained to me. "And so, my life was really shaped, as much as any other white American who ever lived, by Black culture." It gave him, he said, a "good start on human rights."

Carter graduated as valedictorian from Plains High School, then enrolled at Georgia Southwestern College and the Georgia Institute of Technology before earning a bachelor of science from the United States Naval Acad-emy in Annapolis, Maryland, in 1946. The same year, he married eighteen-year-old Rosalynn Smith, a native of Plains and freshman at Georgia Southwestern College, announcing to his mother after their first date, "She's the girl I'm going to marry." Rosalynn helped to raise her three younger siblings after her father died when she was thirteen, while her mother supported the family as a dressmaker, Rosalynn often working at her side.

After Carter enlisted in the Navy, he and Rosalynn set about a new life traveling from post to post as he achieved the rank of lieutenant as a submariner while she tended to their three boys. (The Carters' daughter, Amy, would come later, in 1967.) As a bright engineer, he signed on to duty as a senior officer under Captain Hyman Rickover, later an admiral known as "the Father of the Nuclear Navy," working on experimental nuclear submarines in Schenectady, New York. After cancer took his father in 1953, Carter abandoned his promising naval career with a decision to return to Plains to continue the positive influence his "daddy" had made in the community. As long as he was in the Navy, Rosalynn said, "he didn't think he could ever do anything in his life to have impact on people's lives like his father had made."

Adding to its population of 640, the Carters moved back to Plains, where they took over the family's peanut farms and other agricultural assets while operating Carter's Warehouse, an outlet for seed and farm supplies. Carter's active leadership in the community led naturally to politics. Undaunted by obstacles and long odds, he ran for the Georgia State Senate in 1962, going to court to overturn election results when he proved the election had been rigged by a local political boss. Four years later, he was edged out in a bid for Georgia governor, a painful loss he found difficult to overcome. He found comfort by rededicating himself to his Baptist faith, becoming a "born-again" Christian. Propelled by the idea that faith and goodwill could right the wrongs of southern society, he climbed back in the arena and ran for the governorship again in 1970. This time he won, becoming one of a few young leaders ushering in the "New South" as he proclaimed, "the time for racial segregation is over."

Prevented from running for reelection as governor by a one-term limit, Carter set his sights on the presidency. On the face of it, it was an audacious proposition; Carter was different, a little-known one-term governor and Washington outsider vying for the Democratic nomination against a roster of politically well-established, inside-the-Beltway candidates. Not only that, he hailed from the Deep South, which hadn't produced a president since Zachary Taylor over 125 years earlier. Even his home state's *Atlanta Journal-Constitution* ran a story under the headline "Jimmy Who Is Running for What?"

"Nobody thought I had a chance in God's world to be the nominee," he said.

Carter proved them wrong, winning all fourteen Democratic presidential primaries *because* he was different— a born-again Christian and peanut farmer from Georgia, untainted by Washington, who promised never to lie to the American people. In a post-Watergate, post-Vietnam era, his outsider persona and message resonated. Carter captured his party's nomination as a new brand of moderate Democrat, going on to win the White House in a close election against incumbent president Gerald Ford.

Upon taking office, Carter also showed himself to be a different kind of president. A man of the people, he sought to de-imperialize the presidency, carrying his own luggage, ordering the presidential yacht to be sold, and for a time banning the Marine Band from playing "Hail to the Chief" and "Ruffles and Flourishes" at official events.

With usual intensity, he poured himself into the job, doubling the size of the national park system; negotiating a settlement to give the Panama Canal back to the Panamanian government by 2000; normalizing trade relations between the United States and China; and combating the nation's energy shortage by promoting renewable energy—even installing solar panels on the White House. Then there were the Camp David Accords, his crowning achievement, striking an elusive peace that inspired hope throughout the world.

But there were setbacks. Carter often got in his own way, coming off as prickly and sanctimonious, and clinging to his outsider status to his detriment, refusing to cozy up to the Washington establishment and key members of Congress. Additionally, he earned a reputation for micromanagement, even taking calls on Air Force One to approve the use of the White House tennis courts.

More damaging was the inflation he inherited from the Nixon and Ford administrations and his unpopular decision to boycott the 1980 Olympics due to the Soviet Union's invasion of Afghanistan.

It was the Iranian Hostage Crisis, however, that proved his undoing. In 1978, Iranian "students" stormed the American Embassy in Tehran, taking fifty-two Americans hostage. The crisis wore on throughout the balance of Carter's presidency, leading critics to charge him with being weak and ineffectual, an image reinforced by Desert One, an aborted hostage rescue attempt that resulted in a downed helicopter, the deaths of eight servicemen, and the severe burning of four others.

Carter's hopes of reelection went down with the mission. In 1980, he lost in a rout to Republican challenger Ronald Reagan, who took the popular vote by 10 percentage points. When Reagan succeeded him on January 20, 1981, Carter had been awake for over two full days negotiating the release of the hostages who had been held by the Iranian government for 444 days. A last thumb in his eye: they would be freed in the first minutes of Reagan's presidency.

Exhausted, he and Rosalynn retreated to Plains, to the modest, brick ranch-style home they had built in 1961. After sleeping for nearly twenty-four hours, the ex-president awoke to what he would later describe as "an altogether new, unwanted and potentially empty life."

Unaccustomed to failure, humiliated by the loss, and struggling for a sense of purpose, he had little idea what he would do next.

*   *   *

In his presidential inauguration speech, Carter had invoked his high school principal, Julia Coleman, whose advice had guided him through the years. "We must adapt to changing times, but still hold to unchanging principles," she counseled her students. Slowly, Carter accepted his defeat, adapting to the unwelcome changes in his life, but he held fast to the principles of his Christian faith, emulating, as much as possible, "the perfect life of Jesus, the Prince of Peace." While he had been able to "keep the peace and to promote human rights" as president, he looked for a meaningful way to continue to build on that legacy as a former one.

A year after leaving the White House, he had the answer, awakening in the middle of the night with an epiphany that he could use his presidential library as a dynamic center for conflict resolution. "We can make it into a place to help people who want to resolve disputes," he told Rosalynn. "There is no place like that now."

The Carter Center, as it would be called, launched in 1982, attached to Carter's presidential library in Atlanta, with a goal of focusing on humanitarian issues that had gone unaddressed in the international community by the United Nations, other nations, and nongovernmental institutions. Its eventual success would owe to the qualities Carter had brought to bear in earlier triumphs—his Christian missionary's altruistic zeal, problem-solving engineering mind, boundless energy and steely determination, and close partnership with Rosalynn.

As Carter originally envisioned, conflict resolution became a key component of the center's work, with Carter himself overseeing peacemaking efforts throughout the world. President Bill Clinton, recognizing his predecessor's skill as mediator, tapped him to negotiate an end to North Korea's nuclear weapons program with the rogue state's dictator Kim Il Sung in 1994. Later in the same year, Clinton dispatched him to Haiti as the head of a US delegation to restore the Haitian president to power after a military coup, preventing an imminent US military intervention. The successful outcome of those talks brought Carter to a new level of international prominence and prestige as an ex-president.

Additionally, the center would promote democracy throughout the world, monitoring 115 elections in 40 countries during Carter's lifetime.

Fighting disease, especially those designated by the World Health Association as "neglected tropical diseases," would become another major focus for the center. Among its signature accomplishments are ongoing efforts to combat Guinea worm disease and river blindness, two pervasive maladies little known outside the third world, leading to their near eradication. To oversee the work, the Carters traveled to the most remote corners of the earth where local inhabitants had rarely seen anyone from a first-world nation, let alone a former president and first lady. "We work with the poorest, most isolated people in the world," Rosalynn said. "And if we weren't there, there would be no one to help them." The Carters labored just as tirelessly to ensure the Carter Center's future, raising a billion-dollar-plus endowment.

Separate from his efforts on behalf of the Carter Center, Carter became deeply involved with Habitat for Humanity. His first major outing with the organization came in early September 1984, when he and Rosalynn joined a group of volunteers on a weeklong work project in lower Manhattan's Alphabet City, rehabilitating a six-floor tenement building in one of the city's worst slums to create affordable housing for nineteen low-income families. The image of a former president donning a hard hat and overalls and wielding a hammer in the late summer heat fired the public imagination, providing a stark contrast to the materialism and Wall Street greed that marked the 1980s zeitgeist. It also proved a public relations boon for Habitat, which saw volunteerism skyrocket. In successive years, Carter lent his name, time, and labor to the Jimmy Carter Work Project, weeklong "Blitz Builds" staged throughout the world resulting in the creation of over four thousand homes through 2019.

Even Sunday was rarely a day of rest for Carter, who taught Sunday school at Plains's unassuming Maranatha Baptist Church when his obligations didn't require him to be elsewhere.

In 2002, twenty-one years after waking up to an uncertain, potentially bleak future, Carter was roused from sleep with an early morning phone call informing him that he had won the Nobel Peace Prize.

The Nobel Committee cited Carter's "untiring effort to find peaceful solutions to international conflicts, to advance democracy and human rights and to promote economic and social development."

"The bond of our common humanity is stronger than the divisiveness of our fears and prejudices," Carter said in Oslo, Sweden, upon accepting the honor. "God gives us the capacity for choice. We can choose to alleviate suffering. We can choose to work together for peace. We can make these changes—and we must."

Carter bristled at the notion that receiving the Nobel Peace Prize was somehow vindicating. He knew that many would see him as simply a one-term president who lost his reelection but remained proud of his record as president.

"I don't know of any decisions I made in the White House that were basically erroneous," he told me, maybe a little defensively.

But it made little difference to how he wanted to be seen in history. "I'd like to be judged primarily by our work at the Carter Center," he said. "I don't mean to exclude the White House, but in my more self-satisfied moments, I think about our unwavering promotion of peace and human rights."

Just as Carter had been a different presidential candidate and president, he became in his post–White House years a different former president, ultimately setting a standard for his successors to make their marks after their time in the White House. He didn't let the loss of a second term as president stop him from living a life driven by purpose. He moved on and did the hard work—meetings, negotiations, smiles and handshakes; endless travel to far-flung places across the world; counting ballots, studying diseases, and hammering nails—to make the world a better place. That was what mattered.

* * *

In the spring of 2017, my wife, Amy, and I went to see the Carters in Plains. We attended services with them at Maranatha Baptist Church, where Carter, in a gray suit and bolo tie, taught his Sunday school class. Afterward, we all went to lunch at one of Plains's two restaurants, a cafeteria-style eatery serving the local southern fare the Carters had grown up with. It was Mother's Day, and as it happened, a framed photograph of "Miss Lillian" hung on the yellow cinder-block wall behind Carter when we sat at our table.

We hadn't seen the Carters since the former president had been diagnosed with melanoma that had spread to his brain and liver two years earlier. At the time, he had been given just two to three weeks to live. As in so many other times throughout his life, however, Carter had once again defied overwhelming odds. After a six-month regimen of radiation therapy and immunotherapy, a groundbreaking new treatment, the cancer had miraculously dissipated. As we settled into lunch, our conversation turned to the ordeal.

Carter said he hadn't been especially sad when he had been given just a few weeks to live—to his own surprise, he felt "a sort of equanimity about it."

But faced with what he believed to be his last days, Carter, ninety at the time of the diagnosis, made a vow to Rosalynn to cut back on their crowded schedule, which might have worn out those less than half their age.

Rosalynn was relieved—finally, after sixty-nine years of a marriage that had them going full tilt, they could slow down and quietly take in the days to come. Then, as Carter looked at their calendar, reviewing all the things they had committed to around the causes they held dear, he had a change of heart.

"They're all counting on us," he told her.

The schedule remained in place—along with Jimmy Carter's undying commitment to do good.

RONALD REAGAN / OPTIMISM

On the cold, gray fall morning of November 19, 1985, the world watched in anticipation as President Ronald Reagan met with his Soviet counterpart, Secretary General Mikhail Gorbachev, at a twenty-room chateau in Geneva, Switzerland.

It had been over five years since the last summit between the superpowers. In 1979, Jimmy Carter and Secretary General Leonid Brezhnev had emerged from a three-day meeting in Vienna with a tentative agreement to limit nuclear warheads, parting from each other with a European-style buss on the cheek. Critics charged Carter with literally kissing up to the enemy, but the warmth between the two leaders quickly faded. After the Soviet Union invaded Afghanistan in December, Carter wound up pulling the agreement from congressional consideration the following year.

Since then, the Cold War had only gotten colder. After Reagan took the presidency in 1981, tensions between the US and USSR escalated with a dangerous and expensive nuclear arms race. Two years later, when the Soviets shot down a South Korean passenger plane bound for New York after it had drifted into Soviet airspace, Reagan, thought to be a warmonger among the Soviets, condemned the USSR as an "evil empire." The Russian leadership countered that the US had "finally dispelled" any "illusions" that it could be reasoned with, and it looked like superpower relations were at a grave dead end.

But Reagan wanted otherwise. While he had aligned his foreign policy around a clear victory of American ideals over Soviet totalitarianism, he also sought peace, holding to the notion that a face-to-face meeting could result in greater dialogue between the two nations and, eventually, to nuclear arms reduction—even elimination.

Since Reagan had taken office, however, three of Reagan's Soviet counterparts had passed away in quick succession.

"How am I supposed to get anywhere with the Russians," he said. "They keep dying on me."

Then came Mikhail Gorbachev, just fifty-four, representing a new kind of Russian leader—dynamic, pragmatic, amenable to reform and negotiation. He and Reagan agreed to meet in Geneva.

Their summit started promisingly. Shortly into their introductory session, Reagan suggested that they talk privately, just the two of them and their interpreters, without a phalanx of aides surrounding them. They retreated to the chateau's lakeside boathouse.

As they sat by a roaring fire, Reagan started off their conversation with the elixir of an optimist, a joke:

An American and Russian were arguing about their two countries, and the American said, "Look, in my country, I can walk into the Oval Office, I can pound the President's desk and say, 'Mr. President, I don't like the way you're running our country!'"

And the Russian said, "I can do that."

The American, said, "You can?"

He said, "Yes, I can go into the Kremlin to the Secretary General's office, pound on the desk and say, 'Mr. General Secretary, I don't like the way President Reagan is running his country!'"

Gorbachev laughed; the ice had broken. Their two-day meeting would lead to one of the most consequential partnerships of the twentieth century. While there would be bumps in the road, the pair would establish a warm relationship and eventually agree to massive reductions in their nuclear arsenals as the Cold War thawed discernibly.

When asked later what he first saw when he looked into Reagan's eyes, Gorbachev replied, "Sunshine and clear sky."

"We shook hands," he recalled. "He said something. I don't know what. But at once I felt him to be a very authentic human being."

* * *

Sunshine and clear sky. The words aptly captured Reagan's outlook on life. The fortieth president always saw the best in things, beginning with his midwestern prairie boyhood, which he described as "a rare Huck Finn idyll."

The second of the two sons of Jack and Nelle Reagan, Ronald Wilson Reagan was born in Tampico, Illinois, on February 6, 1911. His father, who gave his infant son his Irish roots, thought he instead resembled a fat Dutchman, nicknaming him "Dutch."

A traveling shoe salesman, Jack Reagan's big dreams were compromised by alcoholism. One of Dutch's searing childhood memories was as an eleven-year-old dragging his father in from the winter cold after he had passed out on their front porch, "drunk, dead to the world."

The Reagan family struggled financially at times, compelling them to move to other Illinois towns in his youth, but as Reagan wrote later, "If we were poor, I never knew it."

His buoyancy came from his mother, who told her sons, "Everything happens for a reason"—they might not understand the reason at the time, but eventually they would. Reagan embraced the belief along with his mother's Protestant religious faith and love for theater.

In high school, he played football, acted in school plays, and was elected president of the student body. His optimism was captured in the poem he added to his senior yearbook, which read in part, *We make our life a struggle / When it should be a song.*

The six consecutive summers he worked seven-day

Shortly into their first summit, Ronald Reagan and Mikhail Gorbachev meet privately in a boathouse, Geneva, Switzerland, November 19, 1985.

Michael Evans, Ronald Reagan Presidential Library

weeks as a lifeguard at a local park, where he saved 77 lives, helped him pay for his tuition at Dixon College, then called Eureka College. He got by on gentleman's C's, earning a bachelor's degree in economics in 1932, while once again becoming president of his class, playing football, and acting in school productions.

As the Depression devastated the Midwest, Reagan found work as a radio announcer in Iowa, earning one hundred dollars a month. Hugh Sidey, who would later cover the presidency for *Time*, recalled hearing "Dutch" Reagan's mellifluous, upbeat voice over the airwaves during his youth in rural Iowa. "Life was hard for us, and the Depression seemed endless," he said, "but he managed to give us the feeling that things wouldn't always be that way, that they would get better."

Things got better for Reagan himself in 1937; a trip to Los Angeles led to a chance screen test for Warner Bros. Pictures, which offered him a contract for two hundred dollars a week. A handsome, camera-ready B-movie actor who often played sidekick roles in bigger productions, Reagan would go on to be featured in over fifty movies—from the acclaimed drama *King's Row*, which Reagan considered his finest performance, to *Bedtime for Bonzo*, a zany comedy that paired him with a chimpanzee costar.

He might have been best known for his role as Notre Dame running back George Gipp, aka "the Gipper," in 1940's *Knute Rockne: All American*, in which, before succumbing to pneumonia on his deathbed, he stoically urges Coach Rockne to encourage the team to go out and "win just one for the Gipper."

In "everything happens for a reason" fashion, Reagan's Hollywood training—learning to effectively deliver a line and project a compelling image—would provide an ideal background for his later success in politics. So would the six elected terms he held as president of the Screen Actors Guild (SAG), Hollywood's actors' union, during which he successfully negotiated for higher pay and better working conditions. Reagan held the post during the McCarthy era, a stormy time for the entertainment industry, which experienced a purge of alleged communists, many unjustly. While Reagan declined to name names when he testified before the House Un-American Activities Committee delving into communist infiltration, it would later be disclosed that he did so in secret.

Reagan's first marriage to Academy Award–winning actress Jane Wyman, with whom he adopted two children, ended in divorce in 1948 after eight years. In 1957, he made his last film, *Hellcats of the Navy*, alongside his second wife and costar, Nancy Davis, a fellow studio contract player and the stepdaughter of a prominent Chicago doctor. The two married in 1952 and had two children.

As Reagan's big-screen career faded, he went on to find steady work in television as host of *General Electric Theater* and *Death Valley Days*. By then he had a growing interest in politics, transitioning from an FDR-style liberal Democrat to an "Eisenhower Democrat."

In the 1960s he left the Democratic Party altogether, becoming a Republican and accepting an offer to do a television speech advocating the presidential candidacy of the party's presidential nominee, Senator Barry Goldwater. Goldwater went on to a crushing defeat against the sitting president, Lyndon Johnson, who took 61 percent of the popular vote.

But "The Speech," as it would later become known, was enough to launch Reagan's political career. Backed by wealthy businessmen, he ran for the California governorship in 1966, beating incumbent governor Pat Brown. (Warner Bros. boss, Jack Warner, upon hearing that his former B-movie employee was running for the state's top spot, protested, "No, Jimmy Stewart for Governor. Ronald Reagan for best friend.")

Reagan would go on to win a second term in 1970, developing a national reputation. In 1968, he tried in vain for the GOP's presidential nomination, coming up short again on a second attempt in 1976. By 1980, after fending off a challenge by George H. W. Bush, whom he tapped as his running mate, Reagan's time had come. He campaigned against President Jimmy Carter under the slogan "Making America Great Again," asking voters, "Are you better off than you were four years ago?"

The answer for most was no. Reagan beat Carter in a landslide.

*   *   *

Winston Churchill once observed, "The pessimist sees difficulty in every opportunity. The optimist sees opportunity in every difficulty."

By the dawn of the 1980s, America seemed to have been saddled with difficulties for two decades. The tumultuous 1960s had given way to the malaise of the 1970s. America was in a period of crippling self-doubt. But Reagan saw opportunity, seeking the presidency to achieve a few bold, sweeping goals: to rebuild American pride and home and prestige abroad; reduce taxes and the size of government; and end the Cold War victoriously. As he had said several years earlier, "My theory of the Cold War is simple. We win they lose."

Upon taking office in 1981, he pledged to guide the country into "an era of national renewal" by restoring "our faith and our hope." His ebullient nature helped to make it so. Reagan relished the role of president, reveling in the pomp and circumstance that Carter had stripped away, imbibing every note of "Hail to the Chief" with swelled red, white, and blue pride as though he were on a Warner soundstage. America could rise again, he assured fellow Americans, "we need only believe in ourselves, in our country, and in tomorrow."

If the presidency was "a splendid misery," as Thomas Jefferson once called it, Reagan showed only the splendor, never the misery. "He doesn't let setbacks or disappointments get him down," Nancy observed of her husband.

Part of Reagan's effectiveness as a leader was his ability as an orator. "The Great Communicator," as he would become known, could pull heartstrings, heal, inspire, and motivate. On the fortieth anniversary of D-Day, he addressed a group of Army Ranger veterans who had been the first to scale the cliffs of Pointe de Hoc, Normandy, France, turning the tide of World War II in June 1944.

"These are the boys of Pointe du Hoc," he said, motioning to the middle-aged men who sat before him, now gray-haired and lined with age. "These are the men who took the cliffs. These are the champions who helped free a continent. These are the heroes who helped end a war."

In 1987, when the Space Shuttle *Challenger* blew up just over a minute after takeoff, killing its seven-member crew, Reagan memorialized them by saying, "We will never forget them, nor the last time we saw them, this morning, as they prepared for their journey and waved goodbye and slipped the surly bonds of earth to touch the face of God."

The same year, he stood before the Berlin Wall dividing West Germany from Soviet-controlled East Germany, indignantly demanding, "Mr. Gorbachev, tear *down* this wall!"

Reagan used his gift for oratory to convey the America he saw. Often he talked of America as "a shining city on a hill," a metaphor for the idealized vision of America he saw, "a tall, proud city built on rocks stronger than oceans, wind-swept, God-blessed, and teeming with people of all kinds living in harmony and peace." One could believe in America's greatness and goodness because *he* believed it.

As Gorbachev had seen in Geneva, part of Reagan's sunny appeal was his gentle, infectious humor. His quips—delivered with a tilt of his head and lilt in his voice, a crooked smile, and a gleam in his eye—could help to make a point or make a friend. Knowing their value, Reagan scribbled one-liners on a catalog of note cards, drawing on them often when a situation warranted.

"As long as there are final exams there will be prayer in schools."

"People who think a tax boost will cure inflation are the same ones who believe a drink will cure a hangover."

Even in the darkest of times, his sense of humor remained intact. Just sixty-nine days into his presidency, when he was shot in an assassination attempt and rushed into a hospital with a nearly fatal wound from a bullet that landed an inch from his heart, he handled it with buoyant grace that captivated Americans. As he was wheeled by gurney into the hospital, he borrowed a line boxer Jack

Dempsey used after losing a championship bout, reportedly telling Nancy, "Honey, I forgot to duck."

Upon being moved urgently into the operating room where a team of doctors awaited him, he quipped, "I just hope you're all Republicans." (One of them, a liberal Democrat, replied, "Today we're all Republicans, Mr. President.")

Reagan's approval ratings soared in the days afterward.

He also used humor to great effect in his reelection bid in 1984. At the first of two debates with his fifty-six-year-old Democratic opponent, former vice president Walter Mondale, the seventy-three-year-old Reagan stumbled incoherently at times, raising questions about his mental acuity.

In the second debate, he deflected them by firmly stating, "I am not for political purposes going to exploit my opponent's youth and inexperience."

Even Mondale laughed. Reagan would go on to win in a walk, taking 49 of 50 states.

His iconic reelection TV ad stated, "It's morning in America," alluding to the bright dawn that had come with Reagan's presidency. There was reason for optimism. The four summits Reagan had with Gorbachev in his second term added to the brightness.

"There was genuine chemistry" between the two men, Nancy Reagan told me.

While supporting anticommunist movements to

counter Soviet expansion, Reagan strived for "peace through strength" in negotiations with his Soviet counterpart. It helped that he could be trusted. As Gorbachev explained to me, he differed from his Soviet predecessors because he "said and did the same thing."

The leaders forged a bilateral commitment to eliminate intermediate-range nuclear missiles, marking the first time the two sides agreed to a reduction in their arsenals and lessening the chance of unthinkable nuclear holocaust. All told, more than 2,600 American and Soviet nuclear weapons would be dismantled.

Additionally, just before Reagan left office, Gorbachev announced his intention to withdraw 500,000 Soviet troops and 10,000 tanks from Eastern Bloc nations under Soviet control.

The world seemed safer. While Reagan would later get undue credit by many for winning the Cold War, his military escalations and aggressive peace-through-strength policies triggered the USSR's inevitable decline as the Soviet empire began to collapse of its own weight.

To be sure, Reagan's boundless optimism and conservative policies had their downsides. He often ignored inconvenient truths that got in the way of a rosier outlook. After his initial denials, it was revealed in his second term that his administration had been secretly and illegally selling arms to Iran to free US hostages held in

Lebanon and using that money to fund an anticommunist uprising in Nicaragua.

Despite the promise of making government smaller, deficits spiked nearly threefold during his tenure—from $998 billion to $2.85 trillion—and his trickle-down tax plan giving breaks to the wealthy under the guise that they would benefit those at lower income levels was never proven an effective means of economic stimulus.

He struck down the Fairness Doctrine, which paved the way for the fragmented, partisan media landscape of today.

AIDS, which ravaged the gay community in the 1980s, went unaddressed by Reagan until late in his second term.

And corporate greed and materialism marked the era, as homelessness, poverty levels, and income equality grew alarmingly. Many felt left behind in Reagan's America.

But Reagan remained enormously popular throughout his tenure in office and, by and large, Americans saw a brighter future for themselves and their children.

"I wanted to see if the American people couldn't get back that pride, and that patriotism, that confidence, that they had in our system," Reagan told ABC's Barbara Walters. "And I think I have."

Poll numbers suggested that he was right. Faith in Americans that the country was going in the right direction jumped from a low of 26 percent in his first days in the White House to 45 percent in his last, and Reagan left the presidency with an approval rating of 63 percent, having changed Washington more than any president since Franklin Roosevelt.

The actor from Hollywood's Golden Age knew the power of a happy ending, and he got one. In his Farewell Address, once again coming back to the image of "a shining city on a hill," he said, "We made a difference. We made the city stronger, we made the city freer, and we left her in good hands. All in all, not bad, not bad at all."

Cut and print.

* * *

In the early 1990s, Reagan was diagnosed with Alzheimer's disease. Friends and family had begun to see it in Reagan's behavior. He wasn't quite the same. He repeated himself; sometimes he forgot where he was.

In Reagan fashion, he disclosed his condition to certain friends by telling a joke about a conversation between two elderly men:

> The first says, "Joe, I have Alzheimer's, but I met a doctor and he's great. You better go see him because you're getting the same thing."
>
> Joe says, "Sure, what's his name?"
>
> The first guy thinks for a long time, and asks, "What's that flower that has petals and thorns?"

"A rose," Joe says.

And the man hollers to his wife, "Rose, what's the name of that doctor I'm going to?"

He let the public know with a letter on behalf of him and Nancy, carefully handwritten in the study of their home in the Bel Air section of Los Angeles in the fall of 1994.

"In opening our hearts," he explained, "we hope this might promote greater awareness of this condition." He continued:

Let me thank you, the American people, for giving me the great honor of allowing me to serve as your president. When the Lord calls me home, whenever that may be, I will leave with the greatest love for this country of ours and eternal optimism for its future. I now begin the journey that will lead me into the sunset of my life. I know that for America there will always be a bright dawn ahead. Thank you, my friends. May God always bless you.

Even at the end of his public life, Reagan's optimism flickered unbridled. Though the gleam may have started to fade, there was still sunshine and clear sky in his eyes.

GEORGE H. W. BUSH / HUMILITY

George Herbert Walker Bush seemed unmoved. Hours earlier, the Berlin Wall had fallen and jubilant East and West Germans were reunited after twenty-eight years of separation. By all indications, the Cold War, which had defined geopolitical dynamics since the end of World War II, pushing the US and USSR to the brink of nuclear war at its height, was fading into history.

Since it had first been erected in the middle of a summer night in 1961, the wall stood as an odious symbol of communist oppression. Two years after its construction, John F. Kennedy spoke at its imposing Brandenburg Gate, proclaiming in solidarity with the throng before him, "Ich bin ein Berliner"—I am a Berliner.

In 1987, Ronald Reagan took his turn at the gate, declaring, "Mr. Gorbachev, tear *down* this wall!"

The West Germans responded thunderously to Kennedy and Reagan as their words echoed a clarion call for liberty throughout the world.

Now the wall was gone, soon to be a relic of the past. Freedom had prevailed.

Yet as he met informally in the Oval Office with the members of the White House press pool on November 9, 1989, Bush was subdued and circumspect, refraining from declaring victory. It was a bewildering reaction to many.

"This is a sort of great victory for our side in the big

East-West battle, but you don't seem elated," CBS's Lesley Stahl challenged him.

"I'm not an emotional kind of guy," Bush replied. "But I'm pleased."

Not emotional? Not quite. As his secretary of state and closest friend James Baker put it, Bush "could cry at the drop of a hat."

Surely Bush was more than pleased. But his restraint, his modesty in a moment of American ascendancy, was intentional; he didn't want to say or do anything that might compromise or embarrass Soviet leader Mikhail Gorbachev, potentially stirring Soviet or East German hard-liners to challenge or oust him as the Soviet empire neared collapse. Nor did he want to alienate Gorbachev, closing the door to further negotiations.

"Bush refused to dance on the wall," Brent Scowcroft, Bush's national security advisor, said. What he was trying to say, Scowcroft asserted, was "Look, nobody lost here. We both win with the end of the Cold War."

When the USSR dissolved with a stroke of Gorbachev's pen two years later, on Christmas Day in 1991, the forty-four-year-long Cold War came to a peaceful end—no shots fired, no tanks in the streets, no bloodshed—a testament, in part, to Bush's humility.

* * *

George H.W. Bush meets with White House reporters in the Oval Office after the fall of the Berlin Wall, November 9, 1989.

David Valdez, George H.W. Bush Presidential Library

Humility had been bred into the forty-first president. "George, don't be a braggadocio," his mother, Dorothy Walker Bush, would chide him. When he came home from a baseball game, boasting of the run he had scored or the grounder he had fielded, she would interrupt with, "How did the *team* do?"

The admonition was part of a broader code in the household of Prescott and Dorothy Bush: If you win, do so with grace; don't boast or self-aggrandize. Give credit to others. If you lose, handle it with dignity. Win or lose, extend your hand to your competitor after the game is over—make a friend if you can.

The lesson stuck. As much as any quality, humility would define George Bush.

The second of Prescott and Dorothy's five children— four sons and a daughter—Bush was born in Milton, Massachusetts, on July 12, 1924, and raised in Greenwich, Connecticut. Prescott was a successful Wall Street investment banker and would go on to serve in the US Senate from 1952 to 1963. Though brought up in establishment wealth and privilege, Bush's parents instilled in George and his siblings a sense of service. That stuck too.

Bush attended secondary school at Phillips Academy in Andover, Massachusetts, an exclusive New England prep school where he established himself as a leader, becoming president of his senior class and captain of his baseball and soccer teams. The country was embroiled in World

War II when Bush graduated on his eighteenth birthday in 1942. That same day, he enlisted in the Navy, training to become its youngest pilot, and going on to serve in the war's Pacific Theater. On a bombing raid over the Japanese Island of Chichi Jima, Bush's Avenger plane was shot down, killing his two crewmates and leaving him stranded in the Pacific, where he was rescued by a US submarine, which popped up miraculously as he drifted perilously toward Chichi Jima and almost certain Japanese capture. Bush emerged from the water believing his life had been spared for a purpose.

While on leave from the Navy in 1945, he married the vivacious young woman whose first name had graced his plane, Barbara Pierce, the daughter of the publisher of popular women's magazines *Redbook* and *McCall's*, whom he had met at a country club Christmas dance four years earlier. After he was discharged, the two moved to New Haven, Connecticut, where Bush attended Yale University, accelerating his studies to graduate with a degree in economics in just two and a half years. While in New Haven, Barbara gave birth to their first child, the future forty-third president, George W. The Bushes would go on to have five more children, including a daughter, Robin, who died of leukemia two months shy of her fourth birthday, a painful loss that rocked the family.

Forgoing a family pass to the riches of Wall Street and a country club life in the Northeast, Bush set out for the oilfields of West Texas, starting on the lowest rungs of the roughneck industry. It was a far cry from the life the Bushes had left in New England. Initially, George, Barbara, and George W. split a duplex in Odessa with a mother-daughter team of prostitutes, sharing a Jack-and-Jill bathroom that they often got locked out of.

Regardless, Bush made his way up in the business, eventually forming his own oil development company, which merged with another firm, then becoming the president of a company selling offshore oil equipment as the growing Bush family settled comfortably in Houston.

But just as his father had done the previous decade, Bush opted to leave a lucrative career for the chance to serve. In 1964, he ran for the US Senate as a Republican in a state then dominated by the Democratic Party. He lost the race but won a seat in Congress two years later, representing Texas's Fifth District and going on to reelection comfortably two years later. In 1970, he gave up the seat for another failed attempt at the Senate. Despite the loss, Bush's rising political reputation landed him an appointment by Richard Nixon as US ambassador to the United Nations, then as chairman of the Republican National Committee. When Gerald Ford took over for Nixon in the wake of Watergate, he made Bush a special envoy to China at Bush's request, then brought him back stateside to become director of the CIA.

Boasting an impressive résumé, teeming with confidence and higher ambitions, Bush sought the Republican nomination for president in 1980. Despite pulling out in front of the pack of other GOP hopefuls by winning the Iowa caucus, the race's first major test, Bush, a moderate, was edged out of the nomination by conservative Ronald Reagan. Much to Bush's surprise, Reagan plucked him from possible political oblivion by naming him as his running mate. Bush would go on to dutifully serve as Reagan's vice president for two terms.

Through his instinctive humility, he engendered Reagan's trust early on. When an attempt was made on Reagan's life just over two months into his first term, sending him to the hospital in critical condition, Bush scrambled back from a trip to Texas to show a smooth continuity of government. When his aides suggested that he go from Andrews Air Force Base straight to the White House by helicopter, Bush rejected the idea, instead landing at the vice president's residence and traveling the two and a half miles to the White House by car. "Only the President lands on South Lawn," he said.

Bush's turn came just under eight years later. He became the GOP standard-bearer in 1988, handily beating his Democratic opponent, Massachusetts governor Michael Dukakis, in the general election. In his Inaugural Address, he expressed his aspiration for America as a "kinder, gentler nation," a reaction, in part, to the harsh excesses of the Reagan years. Looking abroad, he asserted,

"The totalitarian era is passing, its old ideas blown away like leaves from an ancient, lifeless tree. A new breeze is blowing, and a nation refreshed by freedom stands ready to push on."

The breeze blew mightily in Bush's first year in office, knocking down the Berlin Wall. Conservatives scoffed at him for not taking greater rhetorical advantage of the victory. Wouldn't Reagan have traveled to the ruins of the Wall and delivered an uplifting speech about the triumph of democratic ideals over communist tyranny? But by declining to gloat, Bush's relationship with Mikhail Gorbachev wasn't compromised, allowing for ongoing summit negotiations that led to the 1991 Strategic Arms Reduction Treaty (START), which placed limits on intercontinental ballistic missiles between the two countries.

His humble strategy also came into play with the reunification of Germany, plans to remerge West Germany and East Germany, formerly under the Soviet Union's tight control for more than four decades. Bush supported Germany's reunification, including its membership in NATO, against the wishes of Gorbachev, who feared it would strengthen the west's military presence in Europe, shifting the balance of power and increasing tensions with the Soviet Union.

Bush, however, prevailed, negotiating with Gorbachev to allow Soviet troops several years to withdraw from the former East Germany and agreeing that no NATO troops would be stationed there, while providing financial aid to the Soviet Union.

Eventually the Iron Curtain fell, at least figuratively, just as the Berlin Wall had. On December 25, 1991, Gorbachev resigned as president of the Soviet Union, effectively dissolving it as a sovereign nation and releasing its twelve republics as independent states. By the end of the Bush administration the US would recognize all of them diplomatically.

Consensus-building diplomacy was another hallmark of Bush's leadership. He built relationships quietly through small, often poignant gestures—a call simply to touch base or offer support; a handwritten note of encouragement or congratulations; a thoughtful expression of gratitude or friendship.

The relationships he had established with allies across the world through the years came into play in another pivotal moment in his presidency: Iraq's invasion of Kuwait in August 1990 under the orders of Iraqi president, Saddam Hussein, who intended to control Kuwait's vast oil reserves with the prospect of moving against Saudi Arabia.

As the situation in the Middle East played out ominously, Bush was firm in his stance. "This will not stand, this aggression against Kuwait," he said on the South Lawn resolutely as the helicopter blades of Marine One whirled.

In the ensuing weeks, through myriad phone calls and

meetings, he engineered an unprecedented coalition of over forty allied nations around Kuwait's liberation—without opposition by the Soviet Union or China—calling it a "new world order."

After trying in vain to secure an unconditional withdrawal from Saddam through sanctions and diplomatic means, a coalition led by the US, launched air attacks followed by an invasion of Kuwait by ground troops. By March 3, 1991, Iraq had agreed to unconditional terms of surrender. In less than two months, Kuwait was free. The biggest show of US military force since the Vietnam War—425,000 US troops plus 118,000 troops from coalition partners—the Gulf War built American prestige abroad while lifting the stigma of Vietnam that had lingered at home since the mid-1970s.

Once again, Bush led with humility, refusing to spike the football or take credit after the victory.

"This is not a time for euphoria—it's certainly not a time to gloat," he said in a measured tone as he addressed the nation from the Oval Office. "But it is a time of pride. Pride in our troops; pride in the friends who stood with us in the crisis; pride in our nation and the people whose strength and resolve made the victory quick."

Still, despite his singular foreign policy successes, Bush was hampered by domestic policy. During his 1988 presidential campaign, as he accepted the GOP nomination, he assured dubious conservatives that he wouldn't raise taxes. "Read my lips," he said categorically at the 1992 Republican National Convention, "no new taxes!"

It became a Bush catchphrase. Nonetheless, when a 1990 budget deal with Democrats was stalled, Bush capitulated, approving various increases in levees and fees. His backslide, which would later be widely exonerated as an eventual boon to the economy, didn't escape notice. Conservatives were outraged. In his monologue, late-night talk-show host David Letterman barbed that the line should be updated to "Read my lips: I was lying."

Time magazine wrote of *two* George Bushes, one "a foreign policy profile that was a study in resoluteness and mastery, the other a domestic visage just as strongly marked by wavering and confusion."

That latter impression lingered as voters made their choices in 1992. Bush's approval rating, which had spiked to 89 percent after the Gulf War, plummeted as Americans turned their attention from military victory in the Middle East and the Cold War's peaceful end to kitchen-table issues as the economy sputtered. By the summer of 1992, as the Democrats had crowned their presidential nominee, Arkansas governor Bill Clinton, the number had fallen to 29 percent.

A gifted politician, Clinton exploited the growing view of Bush as being out of touch, even unconcerned, with the issues of everyday Americans. The entry of Dallas businessman H. Ross Perot as an independent candidate further hurt Bush's prospects.

Bush, who had conceded that he lacked "the vision thing," ran an uninspired campaign, never able to communicate a compelling narrative for how he intended to lead the nation forward.

On Election Day, he pulled 37 percent of the vote, versus 19 for Perot and 43 for Clinton, who scored a decisive Electoral College win.

*　*　*

Crushed by the denial of a second term, Bush was humble even in defeat. Instead of wallowing in self-pity, he thought about those in his administration who were also feeling the pain of his loss. As a morale booster, he invited *Saturday Night Live*'s Dana Carvey to entertain the White House troops with a surprise East Room performance. Carvey delivered his signature impression of the president, explaining that imitating Bush was a combination of John Wayne and Mr. Rogers.

"Put them both together and you get George Herbert Walker Bush," he said as laughter filled the room and the gloom melted away.

*　*　*

Bush's humility was also evident when it came time to leave the White House. One of his last acts as president was penning a handwritten letter to Clinton, which he left on the Resolute Desk.

"You will be <u>our</u> President when you receive this note," he wrote. "I wish you well, I wish your family well. Your success is our success. I'm rooting hard for you."

The gesture was "profoundly moving" to Clinton, who told me it was "vintage George Bush . . . trying to be a citizen in the highest sense of the word."

Eight years later, when George W. Bush succeeded Clinton to become the forty-third president, his father characteristically put his own ego in check. While there was wide speculation that "41" was offering "43" presidential advice and guidance as his son took up residence in the White House, the reality was that he held back.

"Look, we had our chance," he would say. "Now it's his turn."

It was in large measure *because* he had held the presidency that Bush didn't tender advice more readily, confident that his son didn't need one more voice telling him what to do.

"I don't want to be the father calling all the time," he said.

When he did reach out, it wasn't to provide unsolicited counsel but relief—often comic—from the stresses he knew his son was feeling. One fax he sent to his son, placed in an envelope by a West Wing aide and urgently taken to the president in the Oval Office, contained a joke about a man who was faced with sentencing by a judge after stealing a can of peaches. When the judge sentenced him to six days in jail, correlating to the number of peaches in the can, the thief's wife yelled from the courtroom, "He stole a can of peas, too!"

When a devastating tsunami hit Southeast Asia, 43 asked his dad to team up with Bill Clinton to help toward humanitarian relief. Despite their former rivalry, Bush stepped up immediately. The two ex-presidents—"the odd couple" as they would become known—formed a surprisingly close friendship, teaming up again when Hurricanes Katrina and Rita struck the Gulf Coast. Bush called their relationship "a dividend" in his life, speculating that he may have been the father that Clinton never had. His children took to calling Clinton their "brother from another mother," and Clinton joked that his unofficial adoption reflected the lengths to which the Bush dynasty would go "to have another President in the family."

Dynasty was one of those aggrandizing words Bush shied away from. So was legacy—the "L-word" he called it.

He had no interest in "directing history," declining to crow about his record, host or attend conferences on his administration, or write a presidential memoir, lucrative and often self-serving staples for former presidents.

Instead he was content to leave all that to others. Maybe it was his mother's admonishment—"George, don't be a braggadocio"—still ringing in his ears.

A politician distinguished by humility is like a sun shower—it happens occasionally but rarely escapes notice because it's so unusual. Bush's humility was genuine, as were his thoughtfulness and decency. He was a beacon of character, which came to bear in his most significant accomplishments.

A well-known quote, often misattributed to Lincoln, states, "Nearly all men can stand adversity, but if you want to test a man's character, give him power." As much as any American president, Bush stood the test.

*   *   *

In June 2018, in what would be the final summer of his life, Amy and I visited Bush at Walker's Point, the rambling Bush family compound on the craggy coast of Kennebunkport, Maine. We had seen him at Walker's Point a number of times through the years, including five years earlier after Bush had shaved his head to show his support of the leukemia-stricken son of one of the members of his Secret Service detail who had lost his hair to radiation therapy. A photo of the two-year-old boy sitting on the eighty-nine-year-old's lap, both in matching blue golf shirts as hairless as cue balls, quickly became a viral sensation on social media, a twilight reflection of Bush's quiet caring.

That final summer in Maine, Bush had slowed down considerably. Ailing and newly widowed—Barbara had died two months earlier—he had invited us to lunch and asked me to read him portions of my recently published book, *The Last Republicans: Inside the Extraordinary Relationship Between George H. W. Bush and George W. Bush*. Given his graciousness and failing health, he also likely wanted to give us a chance for a final goodbye.

We sat out on the home's back patio under a cloudless sky in the early afternoon, the dark, sun-speckled Atlantic Ocean churning before us. Despite his wariness about the "L-word," I had chosen to read the book's second-to-last chapter, summarizing my view on how history, given perspective and the distance of years, was coming around to him and his consequential presidency. I read the pages aloud as Bush turned his face upward, absorbing the summer sun.

"Time would be a friend to George H. W. Bush," I said as the chapter wound down:

> Two decades after leaving office, he would begin to be recognized for his sheer competence as President during a seminal time, credited for his incisive foreign-

policy mind, diplomatic facility, and steady, prudent hand as commander-in-chief. . . .

Moreover, in a barbed, self-aggrandizing age when passion all too often overcame reason, America came to value 41's character. . . . In the unexpected warmth of his winter years, the public servant who called for a "kinder, gentler" nation got a little of it back.

When I finished reading, Bush's eyes were closed, his head still tilted toward the sky. For a brief moment, we sat in silence as the waves plunged into the rocks beneath us. I thought he might have drifted off to sleep.

Then, eyes still shut, the humble ninety-four-year-old former president said softly, "That's a lot about me."

BILL CLINTON / RESILIENCE

Y ou'll be president someday," your doting mother tells you.

She's not alone. Time and time again throughout your young life, you hear it from plenty of others too. It suits you.

A Rhodes scholar from humble Arkansas origins, you're a natural politician with a bigger-than-life persona that matches your outsize ambitions and ability.

After leaving home to attend Georgetown, Oxford, and Yale Law School, you come back home to Arkansas with an eye toward elected office.

Why politics? Because, you say, it's "the only track I ever wanted to run on."

You want to serve and make a difference in people's lives.

So, you run. First in a failed race for Congress in 1974, followed two years later by a successful campaign to become Arkansas's attorney general.

Then, in 1978, you win the state's top post, becoming governor at thirty-two, the youngest in the state's history. You become known as the "Boy Governor"—in a *good* way.

Things start off well. As you and Hillary, your wife and political partner, look toward your future, anything is possible—even the presidency.

Then you run into trouble. When hundreds of Cuban

refugees escape from Arkansas's Fort Chafee, where they're being detained, it stirs widespread fear and chaos throughout the state. Though you have little to do with the mishap, it reflects poorly on your administration. A bigger factor is the wildly unpopular motor vehicle tax that you put into place to fund road improvements, raising outrage among constituents.

When it comes time to vie for another two-year term, your opponent, Frank White, a businessman and former banker, rails on your record for mismanagement and fiscal irresponsibility. On Election Day, he beats you in a landslide.

Overnight, you go from being the youngest governor in *Arkansas* history to the being the youngest *former* governor in *American* history.

It wasn't supposed to happen like this. You're devastated. At age thirty-four, your political prospects have been derailed and your future is in doubt. As you put it, you're "almost as popular as the plague."

"What now?" people ask. You tell them, "I'm gonna start working for the next time."

You get back on the track. You go through the shoe boxes and wooden card catalog files that store the well-worn three-by-five index cards of some ten thousand people you've met through the years; you make calls and pay visits; you travel throughout the state to win back the voters. You know you have a chance of winning when one

Arkansan says he'd consider supporting you again after voting against you because of the vehicle tax.

"Why?" you ask.

"Because I figure now we're even," he says.

In a rematch with White, you win by nearly 10 percentage points. You take back the Governor's Mansion, which you occupy until trading up to the White House a dozen years later.

After you've become the forty-second president, you explain your trademark resilience by comparing yourself to the gigantic, dimwitted cartoon duck of the 1950s.

"I'm a lot like Baby Huey," you submit. "I'm big, fat, and ugly. But if you push me down, I keep coming back. I never go away."

* * *

Resilience would prove an indispensable trait for Bill Clinton throughout his eventful and often turbulent life.

He was born William Jefferson Blythe VI on August 19, 1946—fittingly in the Arkansas town of Hope—the first child of the spirited Virginia Cassidy Blythe, who would go on to become a nurse-anesthesiologist. Three months before his birth, his father, William Jefferson Blythe, died in a car accident at age twenty-eight, leaving the son he would never know with a sense that he would need to live a life big enough for both of them.

When Bill was four, Virginia married Roger Clinton, whose last name he would take in a show of support for his little brother, Roger Clinton Jr., born to Virginia and Roger in 1956.

The family moved to Hot Springs, an Arkansas resort town, where virtue and Baptist godliness stood alongside decadence and moral turpitude, a metaphor for the contradictory, complicated formative years Bill would spend there—and for his own emerging psyche.

Roger Clinton Sr. was a car salesman whose physical and mental abuse, fueled by his alcoholism, beset the Clinton household. Bill often played the role of defender of his mother and brother, putting himself between them and his menacing stepfather to protect them and try to make peace.

"My outward life was filled with friends and fun, learning and doing," he wrote. "My inward life was full of uncertainty, anger and dread of ever-looming violence."

Perhaps to outrun the dark forces, he was, by his own telling, "always in a hurry," even when he didn't know where he was going, intent on making his external life "as good as possible."

It explained his evolving "passion for public service" and "deep sympathy for the problems of other people." Politics would be a natural outlet. His interest in pursuing a career in public service came in his midteens. In 1963, as a delegate of Boys Nation, he visited the White House, elbowing his way through a crowd of his peers to press his hand into that of John F. Kennedy, who greeted them in the Rose Garden. The brief handshake and reflected presidential aura made a deep impression on the teenager. In keeping with Kennedy's declaration in his Inaugural Address, "Ask not what your country can do for you, ask what you can do for your country," Clinton decided he would devote himself to public service with an aim "to make things better for people."

A young man of singular talents, Clinton was popular, gregarious, and hardworking. He played the saxophone in the high school band, idolized Elvis Presley, read voraciously, and soared academically. In 1964, he accepted scholarships to Georgetown, then a Rhodes scholarship to Oxford. After returning stateside, he attended Yale Law School. There he met Hillary Rodham, an Illinois native and fellow law student whose talents and ambitions aligned with his own. Following her heart, she moved with him back to Arkansas to launch his political career. They married in 1975. Just over three years later, Bill and Hillary were living in the Governor's Mansion that would eventually be home to their daughter, Chelsea, born in 1980.

Yet the governorship was just a stepping stone as he looked for an opportune time to contend for the White House. His youth and ability led to an invitation to deliver the keynote address at the 1988 Democratic National Convention.

Things didn't go as expected. What started off as a golden opportunity to prove himself in the national spotlight turned out to be a national embarrassment. Clinton, an exceptional but loquacious speaker, failed to win over the crowd, which wanted only to hear from its party's presidential nominee, Massachusetts governor Michael Dukakis. It didn't deter Clinton, who droned on about Dukakis's record. Several attempts to give him the hook—including adding "Please finish" to the verbiage on the teleprompter—went unheeded. The only time the audience erupted in applause was when Clinton wound down after a half hour by saying, "In closing . . ."

Overnight, Clinton became a punchline. On *The Tonight Show*, Johnny Carson quipped in his monologue that "the surgeon general has just approved Bill Clinton as an over-the-counter sleep aid."

Newsweek's much-read Conventional Wisdom column, "CW," opined: "Old CW: president in '96. New CW: he's finished."

Not so fast. Clinton bounced back—and quickly. The following week he appeared on *The Tonight Show* for an interview with Carson, who playfully placed an hourglass on his desk as Clinton sat down.

Clinton took it all in stride, beguiling the audience by

owning his blunder with a string of self-deprecating remarks. "My sole goal was achieved," he told Carson. "I wanted so badly to make Michael Dukakis look great, and I succeeded beyond my wildest expectations."

Carson praised Clinton for being a good sport, and Clinton was back in the game.

Not surprisingly, he threw his hat in the ring for the presidency in 1992, gaining early momentum. *Time* put him on its cover with the subhead, "Why Both Hype and Substance Make [Clinton] the Democrats' Rising Star."

But rising stars can fall just as fast. In January, just days before the New Hampshire polls opened, Gennifer Flowers, an Arkansas employee, alleged in a paid interview that she and Clinton had had a twelve-year affair. Despite Clinton's strong denials, the story caused a sensation, dredging up rumors of other affairs Clinton may have had—"bimbo eruptions," as they became known at the time—which had swirled abundantly in Little Rock through the years.

Once again, Clinton addressed the issue head-on. With Hillary sitting close by his side, he appeared on CBS's *60 Minutes* just after the network had aired the Super Bowl. Forty million viewers watched as Clinton acknowledged "wrongdoing" and causing "pain" in their marriage.

Still, it was Hillary's affirmation that was key. "I love him, and I respect him, and I honor what he's been through and what we've been through together," she said.

"And you know, if that's not good enough for people, then heck, don't vote for him."

It was good enough for many New Hampshirites who gave him 25 percent of the vote in a crowded field. After the results came in, Clinton proclaimed, "I think we know enough to say with some certainty that New Hampshire tonight has made Bill Clinton the 'Comeback Kid.'"

Voters seemed willing to forgive Clinton for his moral failings—or at least to look beyond them. They were taken by his almost superhuman ability to remember names, summon facts, and communicate complex issues simply and understandably. Moreover, they were drawn in by his empathy.

Detractors derided him as "Slick Willie" and mocked him for the "I feel your pain" connection he struck with average Americans. But while it may have been politically advantageous, it was also genuine. He cared. As Clinton biographer Joe Klein put it, "Clinton's public charm— his ability to talk to, to empathize with, to understand: his willingness to fall behind schedule, to infuriate his staff, merely because some stray citizen on a rope line had a problem or a story that needed to be heard—will doubtless stand as his most memorable quality."

The "Comeback Kid" went on to wrest the White House from George H. W. Bush. In January 1993, he became the first of his generation to take the presidency, much as JFK had thirty-two years earlier.

Yet controversy and political adversity lay in wait in Washington too. Clinton stumbled out of the gate, beginning the first months of his presidency with a series of blunders, including a failed attempt at health care reform, adding up to a low approval rating and flurry of negative headlines, including a *Time* cover that featured a tiny image of Clinton and the headline, "The Incredible Shrinking President."

Greater challenges came when a special counsel was appointed by Congress to investigate Clinton's alleged financial improprieties surrounding a real estate investment in Arkansas called Whitewater.

When it turned up empty, Ken Starr, the zealous special prosecutor, morphed his efforts into a politically motivated investigation over a series of other allegations, some unrelated to Whitewater.

As the investigations continued, Clinton forged ahead, pursuing a strategy of "triangulation" in which he adopted moderate policy positions that were neither liberal nor conservative but somewhere in the middle of the political spectrum—often outflanking the opposition by taking their policies and advocating them as his own. The approach worked in racking up a slate of legislative wins that improved American life, including the Earned Income Tax Credit, the Family Medical Leave Act, welfare reform, and the North American Free Trade Agreement (NAFTA), which he signed into law flanked by a bipartisan trio of former presidents, George H. W. Bush, Jimmy Carter, and Gerald Ford. All the while, the economy ticked along.

In 1996, Clinton breezed into a second term, roundly defeating his challenger, veteran senator Bob Dole, and becoming the first Democrat to win two consecutive election victories since FDR sixty years earlier.

But all was not rosy for Clinton himself. Early in 1998 came charges from Ken Starr that Clinton had had an illicit affair with Monica Lewinsky, a twenty-two-year-old White House intern.

As scandal rocked the White House, a national soap opera played out. At first Clinton stridently denied the affair, angrily insisting that he "did not have sexual relations with that woman, Ms. Lewinsky."

Then, as pressure and evidence mounted, he came clean, acknowledging that his relationship with Lewinsky was "wrong," adding, "I misled people, including even my wife. I deeply regret that."

Republicans smelled blood. Even though three-quarters of Americans supported a congressional censure of Clinton over an impeachment, House Republicans went forward with proceedings making Clinton the first president to be impeached since Andrew Johnson in 1868. Despite acquittal in the Senate trial that followed, it was an indelible stain on Clinton's presidency.

Damaged but not deposed, Clinton kept his head down

Nearly two years after his impeachment, Bill Clinton greets a crowd at a rally in Los Angeles, November 2, 2000.

David Hume Kennerly, Center for Creative Photography, University of Arizona

and focused on working toward the good of the country, a posture rewarded by the American people who gave him a peak post-impeachment approval rating of 73 percent. They recognized his flaws and questioned his moral judgment, but they *liked* him. Moreover, they thought he was doing a good job in enacting policies that were paving the way toward the strongest sustained economic cycle in American history—record job growth, a spike in median household income, an increase in the minimum wage, and the lowest unemployment rate in over thirty years.

In fact, the political backlash came at the expense of the GOP, who voters saw as petty and partisan.

Clinton completed the balance of his second term, leaving office in 2001 as peace prevailed, the economy roared, and four consecutive annual federal budget surpluses had been delivered, marking the only time the US hasn't incurred a deficit in over fifty years.

"I'll leave the presidency more idealistic, more full of hope than the day I arrived," he said as his term ended.

On balance, Americans were more hopeful too. As he left the White House, his approval rating stood at 64 percent, the highest of any outgoing president in modern history.

* * *

"There are no final victories in politics," Bill Clinton often says, almost as a mantra.

As much as anyone, he may be reminding himself. But Clinton's career tells us there are no final defeats in politics either—or in life.

As he faced adversity, even of his own doing, Clinton always pushed forward and came back, never letting defeat—or his worst traits or deeds—define him.

He accepted his losses, learned from them, and went on to try to do his best for the people he was serving. Pulitzer Prize–winning historian Taylor Branch, a former Clinton roommate, observed, "he could speak almost fondly of his own defeats, seemingly because he had a prime seat to examine them in retrospect."

Part of his resilience was that he rarely clung to bitterness. Hillary often joked that he forgot who he was supposed to be mad at. It was a useful amnesia, allowing him to move forward unconstrained by passions, an especially practical tool in the transactional world of politics.

Yet it didn't always come easy. In March 1998, as the Lewinsky scandal seethed in the US and the threat of impeachment loomed, Clinton took a nine-day trip to Africa. It included a visit with his friend South African president Nelson Mandela, who took Clinton to Robben Island Prison, five miles off the mainland. Mandela had been incarcerated in the prison for eighteen years of a twenty-seven-year sentence—including a year and a half in solitary confinement—for leading the anti-apartheid movement bucking legal segregation oppressive to South

Africa's majority-Black population. He showed Clinton the quarry where he worked hard labor seven days a week crushing limestone, and his cramped eight-by-seven-foot cell that had been appointed with only a steel bed, thin sleeping pad, and small sanitation bucket.

Clinton asked him if he hated his captors.

"Yes," Mandela replied, but explained that they could strip him of everything except his mind and heart. "Those things they could not take away without my permission. I decided not to give them away."

Alluding to Clinton's political enemies back in Washington, he smiled softly, adding, "And neither should you."

Clinton followed up by asking if he hated his captors after he was released. Mandela replied that for a moment he did but realized that if he continued to be consumed by hate, they would still have him.

"I wanted to be free, so I let it go," he added. Again, he smiled pointedly at Clinton.

Eight months later, in January 1999, Republican House Judiciary Committee chairman Henry Hyde, who had successfully led Clinton's impeachment proceedings in the House, asked for a meeting with Clinton to discuss the impending Senate trial at which Hyde would serve as chief prosecutor. Clinton's aides were appalled. Why would the president meet with the very person who was trying to do him in?

But mindful of Mandela's counsel, Clinton obliged.

"It's my job to do it," he explained. "He's a member of Congress—and a senior member."

A meeting was arranged. After a brief but cordial exchange with the president, Hyde left the Oval Office. As far as Hyde knew, Clinton recalled, "I did not even remember what happened."

Then Bill Clinton went back to doing the work of the American people.

GEORGE W. BUSH / GIVING BACK

George W. Bush's head was pounding. The previous evening, he, his wife, Laura, and a group of close friends had gathered to celebrate his fortieth birthday during a weekend getaway in Colorado. Their dinner turned into long hours of repeated cocktail rounds punctuated by drunken, rambling toasts. Now he was paying the price, even halting his daily three-mile morning jog as his temples continued to throb.

It was an all-too-familiar routine. Drinking was a cultural staple in Midland, Texas, where he had been raised and was trying to make his way in the oil business, much as his overachieving father had before him. He actively imbibed "the four B's"—beer, bourbon, and B&B, an after-dinner liqueur—often in one sitting. Booze-soaked nights frequently turned into early morning hangovers.

But this time he had reached "an inflection point." Drinking, he realized, had become "a priority," crowding out his energies, sometimes turning his good-natured quips into scathing barbs. There had been times in his life when he had "lived a little too large," and now it had become too much. In a feat of resolve, he quit drinking that day.

Sobriety was part of Bush's quest to become "a better man" as he reached the threshold of middle age. The previous summer, in 1985, he had found spiritual mentorship that changed his life. It spoke to the privilege of being part of the Bush family that it came from renowned evangelist Billy Graham, a friend of his parents, whom he had met during his father's vice presidency at Walker's Point, the Bush vacation compound in Kennebunkport, Maine. Maybe it was a portent too; Graham had served as a religious advisor for every president since Harry Truman.

After Graham and Bush had trodden on a Kennebunkport beach and ventured into the Atlantic Ocean for a brisk afternoon swim, Graham asked Bush if he could send him a Bible; Bush said he would be honored. "There was no lecture, no grabbing of the shoulders," Bush recalled. "And I started reading the Bible. . . . A religious walk began."

The "walk" would set Bush in a new direction. He became more focused, more thoughtful, more intent on making his own mark. "When I was a child, I spoke as a child, I understood as a child, I thought as a child," reads a passage in Corinthians, "but when I became a man, I put away childish things." As Bush conceded later, he could not have quit drinking without faith and surely would never have gone on to become governor of Texas and president of the United States.

But it was a proverb from the book of Luke that would define his life going forward, a "timeless truth" that guided him into public service and resulted in one of the most consequential and often-overlooked policies of his presidency—one that would save millions of lives: "To whom much is given, much is required."

* * *

The first child of Barbara Pierce and George Herbert Walker Bush, George Walker Bush was born on July 6, 1946, in New Haven, Connecticut, where his father attended Yale University after his service in World War II. While "Georgie" was Connecticut-born, he was Texas-made, forging an identity rooted in Lone Star pride and swagger after the family made its way to the West Texas oil patch where he grew up.

At age seven, his halcyon Midland childhood of bicycles and backyard baseball was shattered when his younger sister, Robin, succumbed to leukemia close to her fourth birthday, deepening his relationship with his parents.

The family would remain close as it grew—Bush's siblings Jeb, Neil, Marvin, and Doro, were born between 1953 and 1959—bound by tradition and an ethos that ran through the bloodline to never take for granted their good fortune along with a tacit expectation to make something of yourself: prosper, take care of your family, and find a meaningful way to give back—serve your neighbor, your community, your country.

His father, a well-born, Ivy-league educated war hero who would become a millionaire oilman and later turn to public service and rise to the presidency, set the standard. As the oldest in the family and his father's namesake (minus the Herbert), Bush felt "some sort of expectation" to measure up.

In 1959, the family moved to Houston as Bush's father continued to prosper as the cofounder of a petroleum company. Shortly afterward, his parents sent him off to Phillips Academy, an all-boys prep school in Andover, Massachusetts, where his father had gone before him. While he wasn't able to achieve his same level of academic and athletic excellence, Bush thrived as one of the school's most popular students, learning, as he put it later, to "bloom" where he was "planted."

From there he followed his father's path to Yale, throwing himself into fraternity life, earning "gentleman's C's," and graduating with a degree in history in 1968. As the Vietnam War was fought abroad, he enlisted in the Texas Air National Guard, training to be a fighter pilot just as his father had in the Navy in World War II, though limiting the likelihood that he would see combat in Vietnam.

After his service, he attended Harvard Business School, earning an MBA, then returned to Texas, where he settled in Midland, driven to make his own name in the oil-and-gas sector.

In 1977, just four months after meeting at a backyard barbecue, he married Laura Welsh, a Midland native who worked as a teacher and librarian in Austin. The two were, as Laura said, "complementary souls"—her quiet and equanimity contrasted by his extraverted energy and gregariousness. They became parents three years later with the birth of twin girls Barbara and Jenna.

Shortly into his marriage, Bush lost a run for Congress, before going back to the oil business, struggling to find the prosperity his father had attained a generation earlier. While he looked for an opportunity to run for public office as his father and grandfather had before him, he conceded in 1989, shortly into his father's presidency, "My biggest liability in Texas is the question, 'What's the boy ever done?' He could be riding on Daddy's name." By then he had an answer, achieving success in Major League Baseball as a minority owner and general manager of the Texas Rangers, raising his profile throughout the state.

In 1994, two years after his father's reelection defeat as president, Bush launched a campaign for the Texas governorship, defeating the state's popular incumbent governor, Ann Richards. Four years later, he earned a second term in a rout, garnering over two-thirds of the vote and spurring conjecture that he would vie for the presidency. In 1999, he made it official, throwing his hat in the ring under a platform of "compassionate conservatism" and going on to win his party's nomination.

He faced the sitting vice president, Al Gore, in the general election—a close contest that came down to the swing state of Florida, which seesawed back and forth between the two candidates with no final call on Election Night. The election's outcome hung in the balance for twenty-seven days. It would be decided in a US Supreme Court split decision upholding a recount that had Bush winning Florida by a scant 537 ballots, providing the electoral votes to take the White House.

Bush was sworn into office in January 2001, invoking the Bible in his inauguration speech, in which he stated, "America, at its best, is compassionate. . . . When we see a wounded traveler on the road to Jericho, we will not pass to the other side."

He began his term in office uneventfully, hoping to be "the education president," an issue he had pushed successfully as Texas governor. But it was not to be. Just nine months into his tenure, on September 11, America was attacked by members of al-Qaeda, a militant Islamic group, who perpetrated the worst acts of terrorism in US history. Hijacked passenger planes were used as guided missiles to strike the twin World Trade Center towers in Manhattan and the Pentagon in Virginia, while another, on track to hit a target in Washington, DC, was downed in Shanksville, Pennsylvania, after passengers charged the cockpit. Just under three thousand perished in the attacks.

Suddenly, Bush became a "war president," something he didn't anticipate and "never wanted." In the mournful and uncertain days in the wake of 9/11, he rallied the nation, vowing to do everything in his power to keep the nation safe from further acts of terrorism, and earning a soaring job approval rating of 90 percent.

As he brought Americans together around common values, Bush took care not to foment division by scapegoating America's Muslim population. He visited a mosque in Washington and read from the Quran, explaining, "The face of terror is not the true faith of Islam. . . . Islam is peace."

War against the perpetrators of 9/11, though, was inevitable. Bush sent US troops to Afghanistan, whose Taliban government was financially supported by al-Qaeda, led by Osama bin Laden, an Islamic extremist, in exchange for protection. More controversially, in 2003 Bush declared war on Iraq, where the country's despotic president, Saddam Hussein, was believed by the CIA to have weapons of mass destruction that posed a global threat, a claim that was later proven false.

But in the months after 9/11, Bush was also considering a war of a different kind, a fight to combat the HIV/AIDS virus, which had devastated much of the third world, especially sub-Saharan Africa, where it threatened to eradicate huge swaths of the population. The statistics were staggering: AIDS had killed more than twenty million worldwide. Seventy percent of those afflicted with the virus lived in Africa, and eight thousand were dying daily, leaving fourteen million orphaned children. Less than two percent of the thirty million Africans afflicted with the disease were being treated, which meant that those infected faced almost-certain death as the world largely turned a blind eye.

Bush had expressed skepticism around the efficacy of foreign aid when he campaigned for the presidency, even stating that Africa should "solve Africa's problems." This was different. The United States was a blessed nation, he believed, and had a moral obligation to lend a hand to those most in need, especially in what could become the greatest humanitarian crisis in his lifetime. "If you believe that America is a force for good," he told me later, "then you're willing to use US influence to affect people's lives."

There was also a national security justification. "My thinking was significantly affected by 9/11," he explained. "I clearly saw the ideological conflict we faced with our enemy." If the most powerful nation on earth stood idle as an entire continent was ravaged by disease, it would mean hopelessness and resentment—and more extremism and violence. "You've got to be pretty hopeless to become a suicide bomber," he reasoned.

Bush dispatched the government's top doctor of infectious diseases, Anthony Fauci, to Africa to investigate what kind of impact the US could make. Fauci's recommendation was to allocate $500 million toward the prevention of mother-to-child AIDS transmission. Bush greenlit the plan but charged Fauci and a small White House team including his chief of staff, Josh Bolten, to think bigger. He "wanted to do something game-changing," Bolten said. "Something that, instead of at the margins assuaging everybody's conscience, might actually change the trajectory of the disease."

Eight months later, Bush announced in his 2003 State of the Union address the President's Emergency Plan for AIDS Relief (PEPFAR). The initiative was bigger—*much* bigger, the largest international health program in history aimed at a single disease. He called it "a work of mercy beyond all current international efforts to help the people of Africa." It would entail an allocation of $15 billion over five years toward the treatment of those afflicted with AIDS through lower-cost generic antiretroviral drugs. Additionally, it allowed for the care of AIDS patients, including indigent children, while combating tuberculosis, a leading cause of death for those suffering from AIDS, and malaria, a fatal disease prevalent in sub-Saharan Africa.

Four months later, he signed the 2003 United States Leadership Against HIV/AIDS, Tuberculosis, and Malaria Act, enacting immediate relief to the fifteen countries most vulnerable to the ravages of AIDS, thirteen in sub-Saharan Africa plus the Caribbean island nations of Haiti and Jamaica.

"To whom much is given, much is required," Bush explained in a speech to State Department personnel later in his presidency, as he outlined the administration's policy on PEPFAR.

> It is the call to share our prosperity with others, and to reach out to brothers and sisters in need. . . .
>
> Helping poor nations find the path to success benefits this economy and our security, and it makes us a better country. It helps lift our soul and renews our spirit.

Twice during his presidency, Bush visited sub-Saharan Africa to promote PEPFAR and raise awareness about the ravages of the AIDS epidemic. Other members of the first family also took up the cause. Laura visited the region five times, bringing Barbara and Jenna on different trips, and Jenna wrote *Ana's Story*, a hopeful book about an HIV-positive seventeen-year-old mother in Latin America whom she had met during her work with UNICEF.

Still, PEPFAR got little attention from the public and the press, overshadowed by growing partisan divisions, especially around the war in Iraq. After Saddam Hussein had been deposed by US forces, Bush was widely denounced for offering no clear plan or exit strategy as Iraq descended into chaos and sectarian violence. Regardless, Bush narrowly held on to the White House in 2004, edging out his challenger, Senator John Kerry.

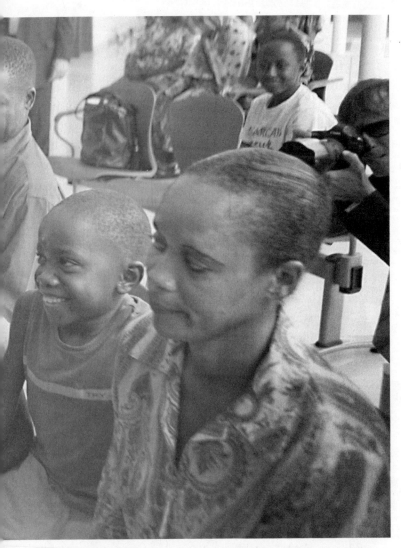

George W. Bush meets with young AIDS patients being treated through the President's Emergency Plan for AIDS Relief (PEPFAR), Dar es Salaam, Tanzania, February 17, 2008.

Eric Draper, George W. Bush Presidential Library

His second term brought additional challenges. In August 2005, Hurricane Katrina ripped through the Gulf Coast, resulting in the deaths of 1,800 and causing $125 billion in damages, making it the costliest natural disaster in American history. Bush was rebuked for his administration's slow and inadequate response to the crisis, which had disproportionately impacted the African American community in New Orleans.

Then there was the financial crisis that came in the last two years of Bush's presidency, the worst economic calamity since the Great Depression. All the while, the wars in Iraq and Afghanistan continued to rage with no end in sight as the toll in blood and treasure continued to rise.

Bush, who had come to the presidency as a "uniter not a divider" and earned overwhelming public support in his first year, saw his public approval rating sink to 25 percent shortly before he left office as the country had become deeply polarized. "I have followed my conscience and done what I thought was right," he said as he bade farewell as president in January 2009.

He could take heart in PEPFAR. By the time he had left office, the program had provided treatment for more than 2.1 million afflicted with AIDS, prevention of the virus's transmission for over sixteen million expectant mothers, and care for another ten million, including four million indigent children. Additionally, antimalaria measures had resulted in the protection of well over twenty million.

As he had foretold in his first Inaugural Address, Bush had shown the best of America as a compassionate nation. When we saw a wounded traveler on the road, we did not pass to the other side.

* * *

Despite his Texas-sized political ambitions, Bush left the presidency with ease. He was content to be out of the spotlight and to settle into a new, quieter chapter in his life. He wrote books, gave speeches, and launched his presidential library and the George W. Bush Institute, a nonprofit focused on policy to "ensure opportunity for all, strengthen democracy, and advance free societies." And to the surprise of many, including Laura, he took up a paintbrush and became a dedicated and prolific painter.

When I've asked him through the years how he thinks he'll be remembered, he's quick to say, "I don't know, but I know I won't be around to see it." He's probably right. His presidency was marked by complex issues and messy outcomes that will take years to sort out as archival records are released, perspective is gained, and passions cool. It's a mixed legacy.

On one hand, he brought the country together after 9/11, and kept us safe despite the murderous intentions of a zealous and diffuse enemy bent on the destruction of America and Western values.

On the other, the costly wars in Iraq and Afghanistan, ultimately aborted, led to the deaths of 4,500 and 2,400 US troops, respectively, and the economic collapse owed at least in part to the deregulations Bush and Clinton had put in place during their administrations.

But often lost in the Bush record is PEPFAR, which has had perhaps the greatest long-term impact. By 2025, the program had saved over twenty-eight million lives—more than the entire population of Australia—a symbol of American humanitarianism on par with the Marshall Plan.

Even Bush's harshest critics had to concede its magnitude. One of them, the *New York Times'* Nicholas Kristof, offered an opinion piece titled "When George W. Bush Was a Hero" to mark PEPFAR's twentieth anniversary in 2023. "You may recall that I spent eight years hammering President George W. Bush for just about everything he did (and he deserved it!)," Kristof wrote, "and yet one more thing must be said: Bush started the single best policy of any President in my lifetime."

George W. Bush deserved that too.

BARACK OBAMA / GRACE

On May 8, 2009, President Barack Obama welcomed an outgoing member of the National Security Council, Carlton Philadelphia, and his wife and two sons to the Oval Office for a farewell meeting and photo. Less than four months earlier, Obama had assumed the presidency under a theme of hope, becoming the first African American to win the White House.

Hope is what his victory represented. How could it not?

Elevating a Black man to our nation's highest office was a sign that our country could overcome its original sin of slavery and deepest roots of racial injustice to live up to its highest ideals. His inauguration had been a day of national celebration and renewal. *Anything* in America was possible. But it was especially meaningful to members of the Black community like Carlton Philadelphia and his family.

Philadelphia's sons commandeered attention during the short visit. Isaac, the elder son, probed Obama on a few policy matters. Then Jacob, his five-year-old brother, asked a question of his own: "Is your hair like mine?"

It wasn't something Obama had been asked before, nor anticipated. He responded by bending his six-foot-two frame over at a 90-degree angle and adjusting his head to Jacob's diminutive height.

"Go ahead, touch it," he said.

Jacob brushed his hand over the top of Obama's head

as the White House photographer, Pete Souza, pressed the shutter button of his camera.

"Yeah," Jacob said, "that's pretty much what I've got."

The photo Souza captured spread virally, a powerful symbol of Obama's seminal presidency. Souza believed that it also said something about Obama's humanity, "knowing what that little gesture meant to that little kid."

For Obama himself, the visit reinforced why he had run for president in the first place. There were the policies, of course; there was much he wanted to do to advance the cause of America, especially for those who stood on the lower rungs of the socioeconomic ladder.

But he also knew that if he were to win, "kids all around this country—Black kids, Hispanic kids, kids who don't fit in—they'll see themselves differently . . . their horizons lifted, their possibilities expanded."

Lyndon Johnson, whose Great Society legislation substantially advanced the cause of civil rights and helped to pave the way for Barack Obama and others, said, "The presidency has made every man who occupied it, no matter how small, bigger than he was; and no matter how big, not big enough for its demands."

That applied to Obama as much as anyone. Yet he carried an especially heavy burden as the first Black president, and it got heavier as the glow of his election faded and a backlash began—a barrage of boldfaced racism that crept into civic discourse, growing louder throughout his

Barack Obama invites
an Oval Office visitor,
five-year-old Jacob
Philadelphia, to touch
his hair after being
asked, "Is your hair like
mine?" May 8, 2009.

Pete Souza, White House

two terms in office. But as in his visit with the Philadelphia family, Obama handled it all with grace, never forgetting that he was the president of *all* Americans.

* * *

To be sure, Barack Hussein Obama's is an *American* story. He was born in Honolulu, Hawaii, on August 4, 1961, at a time when segregation still prevailed in parts of the nation, and as the civil rights movement was beginning to catalyze legal and social change.

"Barry," as he was known in his early years, was a product of the three-year marriage of Ann Dunham, a white Kansas native, and his namesake, Barack Obama, a Black Kenyan, who had met as students at the University of Hawaii. When he was two, his father left Hawaii for a graduate program at Harvard before returning to Kenya, where he would die in a motorcycle accident in 1982 having barely known the son he left behind in America.

Shortly after her divorce, Ann married another University of Hawaii student, Lolo Soetoro, an Indonesian geographer, who moved the family to the outskirts of Jakarta in 1967. Barry spent four years there, first living in a poor neighborhood where he attended a local school with classmates who couldn't afford shoes, before the family left for a more affluent neighborhood where he attended a private Catholic school.

When he was ten, his mother sent him back to Hawaii to live with his maternal grandparents while she remained in Indonesia doing anthropological fieldwork and raising Barry's half sister, Maya, born to her and Lolo in 1970.

Raised in a rich blend of ethnicity, sociology, and culture, Barry groped for identity throughout the latter part of his youth.

"I was engaged in a fitful interior struggle," he wrote of being brought up principally by a white mother and white grandparents, mostly in Honolulu, which lacked a substantial Black population.

"I was trying to raise myself to be a Black man in America, and beyond the given of my appearance, no one around me seemed to know exactly what that meant."

That included him. At times, he felt "utterly alone."

He went to an elite Honolulu prep school, where he achieved some academic distinction, "dabbled" with drugs and alcohol, and played varsity basketball. In 1979, he attended college at Occidental in Los Angeles before transferring to Columbia University in New York.

Slowly he began to find himself, dropping the name Barry to become Barack. After graduating with a degree in political science in 1983, he moved to Chicago to become a community organizer on the city's largely Black South Side, working with low-income residents toward improvements in housing and economic development and finding a sense of belonging. Frustrated by municipal bureaucracy that prevented him from doing more, he enrolled in Harvard Law School in 1988, quickly establishing himself among his peers, who elected him as the first Black president in the 104-year history of the prestigious *Harvard Law Review*.

National notoriety followed, including a book contract to write a memoir, *Dreams from My Father*, in which he offered an unembellished take on his search for identity.

While working as an associate at a Chicago law firm during a summer break from Harvard in 1989, he met Michelle Robinson, an attorney at the firm who served as his advisor, and who had earlier attended Harvard Law School and Princeton University. Their relationship developed into a courtship, and led to marriage in 1992. They settled on Chicago's South Side, where Michelle had grown up, and raised two children, Malia and Sasha, born in 1998 and 2001, respectively.

Declining lucrative opportunities with top law firms after his graduation from Harvard, Obama sought political office, a natural path for one who believed that "we have a stake in one another." In 1996, he won a seat in the Illinois legislature.

Four years later, looking to advance his political career, he challenged a popular incumbent congressman in the Democratic primary, only to get trounced by 30 percentage points. A bigger opportunity came four years later when he vied for and won the Democratic primary for a seat in the US Senate. Buzz about his candidacy and the prospect of him becoming only the fourth Black senator since Reconstruction resulted in an invitation for him to deliver the keynote address at the 2004 Democratic National Convention in Boston.

Delivered on the forty-first anniversary of Martin Luther King's "I Have a Dream" speech at the March on Washington, the speech—just over two thousand words in seventeen minutes—would become life-altering for Barack Obama and his family.

"I stand here knowing that my story is part of the larger American story," he said before a television viewership of just under ten million, "and that, in no other country on earth, is my story even possible." He went on to challenge the cynical notion of an intractably polarized country defined by its red and blue differences, sounding a message of unity and inclusion:

> Yet even as we speak, there are those who are preparing to divide us. . . . Well, I say to them tonight, there's not a liberal America and a conservative America— there's a United States of America. There's not a Black America and white America and Latino America and Asian America; there's the United States of America.

Suddenly he was a national celebrity. Not only did he win his Senate seat with a crushing 70 percent of the vote, but he arrived in Washington as a standard-bearer for the Democratic Party.

But not the only one. Hillary Clinton, the junior senator from New York and former first lady, had cachet of her own and became the odds-on favorite for the Democratic Party's presidential nomination in 2008.

Both declared their candidacies in 2007—first Clinton, then Obama—and both represented the prospect of becoming groundbreaking presidents—Clinton as the first woman president, Obama as the first African American president.

After an often-bitter, back-and-forth battle in successive primaries, Obama narrowly edged out Clinton to become the party's nominee. It was an enormous leap forward—a Black man topping the ticket of a major political party with the prospect of attaining the nation's highest office. Big enough that Obama's campaign slogan, "Yes, we can," contained seeds of hope that could sprawl into a postracial society.

But it wasn't that simple.

The best and worst of America is seen through the prism of race. It reflects our audacious aspirations and crippling contradictions. With attacks on Obama's religion, his citizenship through "birther" conspiracies, and what his political opponents tried to label as "other," the paradox of race in America could be seen clearly in Obama's political ascendance.

Nonetheless, Obama's message won out on Election Day; Obama prevailed, earning over twice the number of electoral votes yielded by Senator John McCain. At a victory celebration in Chicago's Grant Park, the president-elect told a jubilant crowd of over 200,000, "If there is anyone out there who still doubts that America is a place where all things are possible . . . who questions the power of our democracy, tonight is your answer."

That feeling of manifest pride, even elation, that America had turned the corner on race continued through January 20, 2009, when a record 1.8 million people braved freezing Washington temperatures on the National Mall, and 38 million tuned in around the world, to watch Obama sworn in as the forty-fourth president of the United States, his left hand resting on the Bible on which Abraham Lincoln had been sworn into office on the eve of civil war 148 years earlier.

The challenges Obama faced in assuming the presidency were compounded by the burdens he assumed as the first Black president, shared by the Obama family. If they misstepped, it reflected not only on them but on the entire African American community. "We know everything we do or say can either confirm the myths about folks like us," Michelle said, "or it can change those myths."

The key to the civil rights movement had been the hard discipline of nonviolent resistance, championed by

Martin Luther King, which met often brutal aggression with unyielding physical restraint. But it was emotional restraint that was pivotal to Obama's success. "No Drama Obama" faced withering criticism, often disguised as thinly veiled racist taunts, with poise, dignity, and reserve. He never took the bait, kept his cool, and reached beyond himself to achieve a greater goal.

It wasn't easy. Six months into Obama's presidency, Henry Louis Gates Jr., an African American professor at Harvard, was arrested for disorderly conduct by a Cambridge, Massachusetts, police officer responding to a 911 call after Gates tried to force open the jammed front door of his own home despite producing his identification. It was the kind of demeaning situation Obama could relate to, where suspicion and fear was directed at him solely because of his race, regardless of his achievement. Asked about the matter, Obama said that the police had "acted stupidly."

Many moderate whites didn't see it that way. They construed the comment as Obama taking sides; they thought "he was going to be different," and worried he "wouldn't care" about them.

Obama, who insisted that his aides give him unvarnished feedback so he could do his job better, took the comments in stride, relegating his own feelings of resentment and putting himself in their shoes. "That makes sense to me," he responded. He strived to be more even-keeled, determined not to inflame passions but to be a "shock absorber."

In that spirit, he invited Gates and the police officer to the White House to have a beer and talk about ways to establish greater trust between law enforcement and the Black community. While the "Beer Summit" didn't dissipate the dark cloud of prejudice that continued to hover over the country, it showed Obama's good intentions.

The episode became a distraction at a time when Obama was trying to push through the Affordable Care Act, a landmark bill that would create greater health care access and expansion at lower costs. When Obama asked his senior advisor and longtime friend Valerie Jarrett how the other Black members of the White House staff had reacted, she replied, "With all that you have on your plate, they just don't like seeing you being put in this position."

"Which position," Obama joked: "Being Black or being president?"

Distractions notwithstanding, Obama leveraged Democratic congressional majorities to pass the Affordable Care Act, "Obamacare" as it would become known, which would become one of his signature accomplishments. He also enacted a major economic stimulus package, an important step in lifting the country out of the longest downturn since the Great Depression. Additionally, as commander in chief, he greenlit a risky special military operation in 2011 that led to the killing of Osama bin Laden, the founder of al-Qaeda and mastermind behind 9/11, an important milestone in moving on from the horrific terrorist attacks a decade earlier.

His campaign's message of hope and change, however, was a tough sell. There were some who were actively rooting against Obama as expressions of racism became more overt. It became clear early in the Obama presidency that America was far from a postracial reality.

As his honeymoon waned and media coverage of him became more negative, even hostile, Jarrett asked him how he was holding up.

"I'm good," he replied.

"You sure," she asked.

"Yeah, I'm sure," he insisted. "Why? Do I seem different?"

"No." She shook her head. "You seem exactly the same. That's what I don't understand."

But as Obama had discovered about himself during his presidential campaign, things rarely got to him. Depression, he discovered, only set in when he felt "useless, without purpose," and the presidency was rife with purpose—filled with the chance to improve the lives of Americans, comfort those in need, and problem-solve. It allowed him to look beyond the passions of the moment, the pettiness, and racist innuendo and jibes. It made his "heart bigger." "The work, I loved," he wrote later. "Even when it didn't love me back."

There was enough love to ensure Obama's comfortable reelection in 2012, as he easily fended off a challenge by former Massachusetts governor Mitt Romney, a sign of the confidence the bulk of Americans had in his leadership.

Obama saw progress in his second term. After driving through progressive LGBTQ reform, he celebrated a landmark Supreme Court decision in 2015 legalizing same-sex marriage. In the wake of a mass shooting at Sandy Hook Elementary School in Newtown, Connecticut, he signed an executive order requiring background checks for those buying guns at gun shows. And the economy continued to rebound as unemployment dropped steadily.

But the issue of race continued to fester as a spate of racially motivated violence played out. It was seen most plainly in Ferguson, Missouri, which erupted in civil unrest in 2014 after Michael Brown, an unarmed Black teenager, was slain by a white police officer.

Several unarmed Black men were shot by officers in the riots that followed, spawning the Black Lives Matter movement. Largely white detractors countered with the slogan "All Lives Matter," and a Blue Lives Matter movement in support of law enforcement.

"The deepest fault lines of our democracy have suddenly been exposed, perhaps even widened," Obama said after five Dallas police officers were killed by a Black man two years later, adding, "I'm here to say we must reject such despair. I'm here to insist we're not as divided as we seem."

Surely it must have been hard to mask his own despair. In 2015, he spoke at a memorial service in Charleston, South Carolina, for the minister of Emanuel African Methodist Episcopal Church, the oldest Black church in the South, who had been killed along with eight other Black parishioners by a twenty-one-year-old white supremacist during a Bible study class. The president eulogized the minister before pausing at length as he solemnly looked down at the pulpit.

Then, emotionally, slightly off-key, he began singing "Amazing Grace" as the congregation slowly joined in, the sound of hope rising in their voices. "May God continue to shed His grace on the *United* States of America," he closed with spiritual fervor after reading the names of the nine who had perished. It was an emblematic moment for Obama, not just as a heartfelt expression in a time of national pain but because it embodied the singular grace he had shown throughout his presidency.

It helped that Obama took the long view, finding solace in how far America had come despite the racial divisions that flared up in his presidency. He knew that progressive leaps forward are met with regressive pushback before we leap forward once again, ultimately gaining irrevocable ground in an unending quest to become a more perfect union.

"I always tell young people in particular," he said, "do not say that nothing has changed when it comes to race in America. It is incontrovertible that race relations have improved significantly during my lifetime and yours."

As much as anyone, he was living proof.

* * *

Two years before becoming president, Obama wrote that the idea that "one isn't confined to one's dreams" because of the opportunities to realize them is inherent in the American proposition, but "in Black America the idea represents a radical break from the past, a severing of the psychological shackles of slavery and Jim Crow. It is perhaps the most important legacy of the civil rights movement, a gift from those leaders like John Lewis and Rosa Parks who marched, rallied, and endured threats, arrests, and beatings to widen the doors of freedom." Indeed, the doors would open wide enough for Obama to inhabit the White House in 2009.

Five years into his presidency, Obama visited the LBJ Presidential Library in Austin, Texas, to offer the keynote address at the Civil Rights Summit, a three-day conference

I hosted to commemorate the fiftieth anniversary of the 1964 Civil Rights Act. The conference included former presidents George W. Bush, Bill Clinton, and Jimmy Carter, and many of the giants of the civil rights movement.

Prior to his speech, the president, Michelle Obama, John Lewis, and I ascended the stairs of the library's Great Hall—a giant presidential seal carved into its travertine marble—and visited an exhibit featuring "Cornerstones of Civil Rights." The Thirteenth Amendment, barring slavery, and a copy of the Emancipation Proclamation signed by Lincoln hung alongside the Civil Rights Act and Voting Rights Act, signed by Lyndon Johnson, milestones marking inexorable advancement in America's stubborn struggle with race just as Obama's political climb had been.

Shortly afterward, Obama delivered his address to a standing-room-only crowd in the LBJ Auditorium. The office of the presidency, he told the audience, is "humbling":

> You're reminded in this great democracy that you are but a relay swimmer in the currents of history, bound by decisions of those who came before, relying on the efforts of those who follow to fully vindicate your vision. But the presidency also affords a unique opportunity to bend those currents.

As he stood behind the presidential podium, the forty-fourth president personified the vindicated visions of John Lewis and others who had gone before him. Well into his leg of the race, Barack Obama had bent the currents of history not only by attaining the nation's highest office but by occupying it with grace, defying fevered bigotry and dispelling racial stereotypes, and showing what a Black person can achieve—but also, as he surely intended, what America is capable of.

Mark Updegrove, Barack Obama, Michelle Obama, and John Lewis ascend the stairs of the Great Hall during the LBJ Presidential Library's Civil Rights Summit, April 10, 2014.

David Hume Kennerly, Center for Creative Photography, University of Arizona

ACKNOWLEDGMENTS

First and foremost, I am deeply grateful to the presidents in these pages for the interviews, conversations, and interactions through the years that have provided firsthand insight into their character. Likewise, I'm also indebted to the late Betty Ford, Rosalynn Carter, Nancy Reagan, and Barbara Bush, and to Hillary Clinton, Laura Bush, and Michelle Obama.

Thank you to those who have served or continue to serve in the presidents' offices and foundations: Penny Circle, Judi Risk, Gleaves Whitney, Paige Alexander, Deanna Congileo, Beth Davis, Joanne Drake, David Trulio, Jean Becker, Andy Card, Nancy Lazenby, Laura Pears, Jon Davidson, Bruce Lindsey, Stephanie Streett, Angel Ureña, Freddy Ford, Logan Garner, Ken Hersh, David Kramer, Robbin Cohen, Valerie Jarrett, Laura Lucas Magnuson, Michael Strautmanis, and Tina Tchen.

There isn't a better editor than Sean Desmond, who believed in this project and provided invaluable guidance as we embarked on it. I've appreciated our partnership. Also, at HarperCollins, thanks to Jonathan Burnham and Doug Jones, and to Tina Andreadis, Kate D'Esmond, Jessica Gilo, Jackie Quaranto, Michael Siebert, and Leah Wasielewski.

Our presidential libraries, administered through the National Archives under the superb leadership of Colleen Shogan, are indispensable for understanding the modern presidency—I have drawn on their considerable resources in various ways for all my books. Thanks to the libraries and my talented and loyal friend David Hume Kennerly for contributing the photographs in this volume.

At the LBJ Foundation, thank you to friends and fellow trustees Larry Temple, Tom Johnson, Ben Barnes, Elizabeth Christian, Lyndon Olson, Stacey Abrams, Robert Allbritton, John Beckworth, Joe Califano, Julián Castro, Nicole Covert, Tom Daschle, JR DeShazo, Rodney Ellis, Wayne Gibbens, Lloyd Hand, Jay Hartzell, Bill Hobby, Kay Bailey Hutchison, Luci Baines Johnson, Jim Jones, Ron Kirk, Jack Martin, Vilma Martinez, Ed Mathias, Cappy McGarr, Lyndon Olson, Catherine Robb, Lynda Johnson Robb, Evan Smith, Roy Spence, Courtenay Valenti, Casey Wasserman, and Tonya Williams—and to our team at the LBJ Foundation: Adam Brodkin, Sherry Brown, Crystal Esparza, Jay Godwin, Courtney Hughes, Russ Hull, Balmore Lazo, Sarah McCracken, Natalia Morgan, Dan Perry, Eileen Powell, Kevin Solka, Samantha Stone, Jenny Urevig, and my stalwart assistant, Hannah Green.

Thanks to my colleagues at ABC News—Desiree Adib, Andrea Amiel, David Baker, Luca Balbo, Marc Burstein, DJ Cunningham, Linsey Davis, Chris Donovan, Santina Leuci, Diane Macedo, Kat McCullough, Terry Moran,

David Muir, Regan Odenwald, Maria Olloqui, Kyra Phillips, Martha Raddatz, George Stephanopoulos, Carrie Strassberg, Nic Uff, Jim Vojtech, Chris Watson, Justin Weaver, and Kayna Whitworth—and those who have contributed to the success of PBS's *Live from the LBJ Library with Mark Updegrove*—Jim Dunford, Selena Lauterer, Krista Nance, Luis Patiño, and Sara Robertson. Thanks, too, to Monica Abangan at Washington Speakers Bureau.

I've been fortunate to be able to discuss presidents and the institution of the presidency with knowledgeable friends, colleagues, and fellow authors including Ken Adelman, John Avlon, Peter Baker, Melody Barnes, Michael Beschloss, Talmage Boston, Bill Brands, John Bridgeland, Doug Brinkley, Ken Burns, Don Carleton, Frank Gannon, Susan Glasser, Doris Kearns Goodwin, Steve Harrigan, Will Inboden, Bob Inman, Peniel Joseph, Anita McBride, Stewart McLaurin, Bill McRaven, Jon Meacham, Tim Naftali, Lynn Novick, Marc Selverstone, Julia Sweig, Chris Whipple, Lawrence Wright, Andrew Young, Julian Zelizer, and my longtime University of Texas teaching partner, Mark Lawrence.

And I'm lucky to have the support of many old friends including Allison Bacon, Craig Barron, Jean Becker, John Bredar, John Hope Bryant, Marty Dobrow, Amy Erben, Randy Erben, Bill Gurney, Mary Herman, Tim Herman, Steve Huestis, Jim Popkin, Lee Rosenbaum,

Bob Santelli, Nick Segal, Hal Stein, Lawrence Temple, Jeff van den Noort, and Diane Walter—and members of a close blended family: Glenn, Susie, Meredith, and James Crafford; Jim and Nancy Krombach; Elizabeth and Will Oliver; Richard, Kim, Sam, Henry, and Nina Storm; and Skip Wood and the late Sandy Wood.

My kids and their significant others—Isabel and Maggie Lodge, Charlie Updegrove, Mateo Saralegui and Maddie LeBlanc, and Tallie Updegrove—give me great pride, joy, and hope for the future. This book is dedicated to them.

Finally, my love and gratitude to my wife, Amy, who insisted that the speech I've given many times, "Lessons in Character from Seven Presidents," would make a great book. I only hope I've proven her right.

— MKU

Austin, Texas

NOTES

INTRODUCTION

1 "A great man is one sentence": Pico Iyer, "America's First Renaissance Woman: Clare Boothe Luce," *Time*, October 19, 1987.

1 "I am not interested in my place in history": Morris, *The Price of Fame*, 528.

2 "He went to China": John Stacks and Strobe Talbott, "Interview with Richard Nixon: Paying the Price," *Time*, April 2, 1990.

2 "He resigned the office": Ibid.

GERALD R. FORD / DOING WHAT'S RIGHT

8 Ford wrestled with whether: Ford, *A Time to Heal*, 52–53.

9 "Where's your n****r player?": Smith, *An Ordinary Man*, 63.

10 He went on to the University of Michigan: "Growing Up Grand: The Early Years of Gerald R. Ford and the Early Years of Grand Rapids," Gerald R. Ford Library and Museum, FordLibraryMuseum.gov.

10 "we can't really find anything nasty": Ibid.

11 "I'm Dick Nixon from California": Interview with Gerald Ford, Kunhardt Film Foundation, October 22, 1996.

13 "a congressman's congressman": George Will, "In 'An Ordinary Man,' Gerald Ford Emerges with a Certain Greatness," *Washington Post*, March 3, 2023.

13 "He puts one in mind of a big sloppy dog": Smith, *An Ordinary Man*, 293.

14 "a third rate burglary" attempt: "Watergate and the White

House: The 'Third Rate Burglary' That Toppled a President,"
U.S. News & World Report, August 19, 1974.

14   "Can you imagine Jerry Ford in this chair?": "Jules Witcover:
The Nixon Pardon Revisited," *Washington Examiner*, January 1,
2007.

14   "My whole conduct as vice president": James H. Naughton
and Adam Clymer, "Gerald R. Ford Dies at 93," *New York
Times*, December 28, 2006.

15   "the hurt was deep": J. Y. Smith and Lou Cannon, "Gerald
R. Ford, 93, Dies; Led in Watergate's Wake," *Washington Post*,
December 26, 2006.

15   "We can do it": Richard Norton Smith, "First Ladies: Betty
Ford," C-SPAN, December 2, 2013.

16   "I don't think the public": Barry Werth, "President Gerald
R. Ford's Priority Was to Unite a Divided Nation,"
Smithsonian, February 2007.

16   "recovery, not revenge": Erica Felci, "Ford's 'Integrity' Recalled
on Centennial of His Birth," *USA Today*, July 14, 2013.

16   "It's going to cost you": Werth, *31 Days*, 317.

17   Overnight his lofty approval rating: Lydia Saad, "Gallup
Vault: A Pardon That Took a Decade to Forgive," Gallup,
September 7, 2017.

17   "far more serious": Ibid.

17   At home, Ford tried to tame: "Funeral Tributes
and Honors," Gerald R. Ford Library & Museum,
Fordlibrarymuseum.gov.

21   "You're playing into a stereotype, Mr. President": Interview
with the author for Updegrove, *Second Acts*.

21   "That's easy, Mark": Ibid.

21   Two-thirds of Americans stood against: Saad, "Gallup Vault."

JIMMY CARTER / DOING GOOD

24   "We can pack our bags and go home": Wright, *13 Days*, 257.

24   Instead of signing each: Interview with the author, Civil
Rights Summit, LBJ Presidential Library, April 8, 2014.

25   hand-delivered the batch to Begin: Wright, *13 Days*, 258.

25   "Let's try again": Interview with the author, Civil Rights Summit, LBJ Presidential Library, April 8, 2014.

28   "All my playmates, all of my companions": Ibid.

28   "good start on human rights": Interview with the author, "Jimmy Carter Looks Back at a Life of Faith and Service, and Ahead to a More Peaceful World," *Parade*, February 16, 2018.

28   "She's the girl I'm going to marry": Updegrove, *Second Acts*, 154.

29   "he didn't think he could ever": Bourne, *Jimmy Carter*, 80.

30   "Jimmy Who Is Running for What": Jeffrey Frank, "The Primary Experiment: 'Jimmy Who?'" *New Yorker*, May 1, 2015.

30   "Nobody thought I had a chance": Interview with the author, "An Intimate Chat with Jimmy and Rosalyn Carter," *Parade*, November 2, 2013.

31   Additionally, he earned: Ronald Kessler, "The Real Jimmy Carter," Newsmax, April 21, 2008.

32   "an altogether new, unwanted and potentially empty life": Jimmy Carter and Rosalynn Carter, *Everything to Gain*, 3–4.

33   "We must adapt to changing times": Interview with the author, LBJ Presidential Library, February 18, 2011.

33   "the perfect life of Jesus, the Prince of Peace": Interview with the author, "Jimmy Carter Looks Back at a Life of Faith and Service, and Ahead to a More Peaceful World," *Parade*, February 16, 2018.

33   "keep the peace and to promote human rights": Ibid.

33   "We can make it into a place": Jimmy Carter and Rosalyn Carter, *Everything to Gain*, 153.

34   Additionally, the center would promote democracy: "Peace Programs," Carter Center, Cartercenter.org.

35   "We work with the poorest, most isolated": Interview with the author, "An Intimate Chat with Jimmy and Rosalyn Carter," *Parade*, November 2, 2013.

35   His first major outing: "Carpenter Named Carter Comes to New York," *New York Times*, September 3, 1984.

35 In successive years, Carter lent his name: "Jimmy Carter Work Projects," Habitat for Humanity, Habitat.org.

36 "untiring effort to find peaceful solutions": "Nobel Peace Prize 2002," Nobel Prize, Nobelprize.org.

36 "The bond of our common humanity": Ibid.

36 He knew that many: Interview with the author, LBJ Presidential Library, February 18, 2011.

36 "I don't know of any decisions": Interview with the author for Updegrove, *Second Acts*, March 22, 2005.

37 "I'd like to be judged primarily": Interview with the author, "An Intimate Chat with Jimmy and Rosalyn Carter," *Parade*, November 2, 2013.

38 "a sort of equanimity about it": Interview with the author, "Jimmy Carter Looks Back at a Life of Faith and Service, and Ahead to a More Peaceful World," *Parade*, February 16, 2018.

38 "They're all counting on us": Ibid.

RONALD REAGAN / OPTIMISM

40 "evil empire": Andrew Glass, "Reagan Brands the Soviet Union, 'Evil Empire,' March 8, 1983," *Politico*, March 8, 2018.

40 "finally dispelled": George J. Church, "Ronald Reagan and Yuri Andropov: Men of the Year," *Time*, January 2, 1984.

41 "How am I supposed to get anywhere with the Russians": Ronald Reagan, *An American Life*, 611.

41 "An American and a Russian were arguing": "Reagan Tells Soviet Jokes," YouTube, Youtube.com.

42 "Sunshine and clear sky": Morris, *Dutch*, 556.

42 "We shook hands": Ibid.

43 "a rare Huck Finn idyll": Marilyn Berger, "Ronald Reagan Dies at 93; Fostered Cold-War Might and Curbs on Government," *New York Times*, June 6, 2004.

43 "drunk, dead to the world": Barron Youngsmith, "Why Do So Many Politicians Have Daddy Issues," Slate, August 22, 2012.

43 "If we were poor, I never knew it": Ronald Reagan, *An American Life*, 9.

43 "Everything happens for a reason": Nancy Reagan, *My Turn*, 107–8.

43 *We make our life a struggle / When it should be a song*: Ibid., 107.

43 The six consecutive summers: Lou Cannon, "Ronald Reagan: Life Before the Presidency," Miller Center, Millercenter.com.

46 "Life was hard for us": Morris, *Dutch*, 117.

48 "No, Jimmy Stewart for Governor": "California: Ronald for Real," *Time*, October 7, 1966.

49 "The pessimist sees difficulty in every": "Being an Optimist in an Age of Pessimism," TEDxSurrey, TED, January 9, 2022.

49 "My theory of the Cold War": Interview with Will Inboden, "The Peacemaker: Ronald Reagan, the Cold War, and the World on the Brink," Hoover Institution, March 15, 2023.

49 "an era of national renewal": Ronald Reagan, Inaugural Address, January 20, 1981.

50 "We need only believe": Ronald Reagan, Remarks on New Year's Day, January 1, 1982.

50 "a splendid misery": "Founders Online: From Thomas Jefferson to James Madison, 28 October 1785," National Archives, Founders.archives.gov.

50 "He doesn't let setbacks": Nancy Reagan, *My Turn*, 108.

51 "a shining city on a hill": Ronald Reagan, Farewell Address, January 11, 1989.

51 "a tall, proud city": Ibid.

51 Knowing their value, Reagan: "Ronald Reagan's Index Cards of One-liners," CBS News, July 20, 2014.

51 "As long as there are final exams": Ibid.

51 "People who think a tax boost": Ibid.

52 "Honey, I forgot to duck": David Smith, "Honey, I Forgot to Duck: The Reagan Assassination Attempt 30 Years On," *Guardian*, March 30, 2021.

52 "There was genuine chemistry": Conversation with the author, Los Angeles, November 2, 1999.

53 "peace through strength": Lou Cannon, "Reagan: 'Peace Through Strength,'" *Washington Post*, August 18, 1980.

53 "said and did the same thing": Interview with the author, LBJ Presidential Library, October 18, 2011.

53 All told, more than 2,600: Lou Cannon, "Ronald Reagan: Foreign Affairs," Miller Center, Millercenter.org.

53 Additionally, just before Reagan left office: Ibid.

54 Despite the promise of making government smaller: Yergin and Stanislaw, *Commanding Heights*, 341–42.

54 "I wanted to see if the American people": Marilyn Berger, "Ronald Reagan Dies at 93; Fostered Cold-War Might and Curbs on Government," *New York Times*, June 6, 2004.

54 Faith in Americans that the country: "Satisfaction with the United States," Gallup, and "Ronald Reagan and Public Approval," American Presidency Project, University of California, Santa Barbara.

55 In Reagan fashion, he disclosed: Richard Corliss, "The Man Who Changed America," *People*, June 21, 2004.

56 He let the public know with a letter: Morris, *Dutch*, 665.

GEORGE H. W. BUSH / HUMILITY

58 "This is a sort of great victory": Walter Shapiro, "1989–2001: America's Lost Weekend," *New Republic*, June 27, 2022.

59 "could cry at the drop of a hat": Interview with the author for Updegrove, *The Last Republicans*.

59 "Bush refused to dance on the wall": Frederick Kempe, "Brent Scowcroft and the Fall of the Berlin Wall," Atlantic Council, November 2, 2009.

62 "George, don't be a braggadocio": Interview with the author for Updegrove, *Second Acts*.

62 "How did the *team* do": Ibid.

65 "Only the President lands on South Lawn": Peter Grier, "Remembering George H. W. Bush, a Calm Hand in a Turbulent Time," *Christian Science Monitor*, February 21, 2019.

67 "This will not stand": John Gans, "The Costs of George

H. W. Bush's Foreign Policy Genuis," *Foreign Policy*, December 7, 2018.

68 The biggest show of US military force: Morgan Till and Sam Lane, "George H. W. Bush, Nation's 41st President and WWII Veteran, Dies at 93," PBS, December 1, 2018.

69 "Read my lips: I was lying": Lily Rothman, "The Story Behind George H. W. Bush's Famous 'Read My Lips, No New Taxes' Promise," *Time*, December 1, 2018.

69 "a foreign policy profile": George J. Church, "A Tale of Two George Bushes," *Time*, January 7, 1991.

69 Bush's approval rating: "George H. W. Bush Public Approval," American Presidency Project, University of California, Santa Barbara.

70 "the vision thing": George E. Condon Jr. and *National Journal*, "The Bush with 'the Vision Thing' Comes Home to the White House," *Atlantic*, July 15, 2013.

70 "Put them both together": "Christmas Ceremony for the White House Staff," C-SPAN, December 7, 1989, C-Span .org.

71 "You will be <u>our</u> President when you receive": "'Dear Bill': Clinton Reads Heartfelt Letter from George H. W. Bush," ABC News, December 1, 2018.

71 "profoundly moving": Interview with the author, "'Dear Bill': Clinton Reads Heartfelt Letter from George H. W. Bush," ABC News, December 1, 2018.

71 "Look, we had our chance": Interview with the author for Updegrove, *Second Acts*, March 22, 2006.

71 "I don't want to be the father calling all the time": Ibid.

71 One fax he sent to his son: Jean Edward Smith, *Bush*, 658.

72 "a dividend": Interview with the author, "An Exclusive Conversation with President and Mrs. Bush," *Parade*, July 15, 2012.

72 "brother from another mother": Tessa Berenson Rogers, "George W. Bush Says Bill Clinton Is His 'Brother from Another Mother,'" *Time*, November 13, 2014.

72 "to have another President in the family": "Opposites Attract," *Guardian*, June 30, 2005.

72 "L-word": Interview with the author for Updegrove, *Second Acts*, March 22, 2006.

72 "directing history": Ibid.

74 "Time would be a friend to George H. W. Bush": Updegrove, *The Last Republicans*, 400–401.

75 "That's a lot about me": Conversation with the author, Walker's Point, Kennebunkport, Maine, June 19, 2018.

BILL CLINTON / RESILIENCE

78 "You'll be president someday": "Virginia Kelley (1923–1994): The Woman Who Raised a President," *Tampa Bay Times*, January 7, 1994.

78 "the only track I ever wanted to run on: Maraniss, *First in His Class*, 390.

79 "almost as popular as the plague": Ibid., 389.

79 "I'm gonna start working for the next time": Ibid., 390.

79 You go through the shoe boxes: Ibid., 392.

80 "Because I figure now we're even": Orientation film, William J. Clinton Library, Little Rock, Arkansas.

80 "I'm a lot like Baby Huey": Michael Duffy, "The State of Bill Clinton," *Time*, February 7, 1994.

81 "My outward life": Bill Clinton, *My Life*, 149.

81 "always in a hurry": Ibid., 7.

81 "as good as possible": Ibid., 149.

81 "passion for public service": Ibid.

82 "to make things better for people": "Bill Clinton: From the Collection: The Presidents," *American Experience*, PBS.

83 It didn't deter Clinton: Robert Fleegler, "How Bill Clinton Turned a Dreadful Convention Speech into Political Stardom," *Washington Post*, August 18, 2020.

83 "the surgeon general has just approved Bill Clinton": Ibid.

83 "Old CW": Ibid.

84 "My sole goal was achieved": Deborah Christensen, "If You've Got the Time, Heeere's Johnny—and Bill," *Los Angeles Times*, July 29, 1988.

84 "Why Both Hype and Substance": *Time*, January 27, 1992.

84 Forty million viewers watched as Clinton: "The Choice 2016," *Frontline*, PBS, 2016.

85 "I think we know enough to say": John King, "Bill Clinton Returns to New Hampshire," CNN, February 18, 1999.

85 "Clinton's public charm—his ability to talk": Joe Klein, *The Natural*, 195.

86 "The Incredible Shrinking President": *Time*, June 7, 1993.

87 "did not have sexual relations with that woman": James Bennet, "The President Under Fire: The Overview," *New York Times*, January 7, 1998.

87 "wrong": "Testing of a President: In His Own Words," *New York Times*, August 18, 1998.

87 Damaged but not deposed: Drew Desilver, "Clinton's Impeachment Barely Dented His Public Support, and It Turned Off Many Americans," Pew Research Center, October 3, 2019.

90 "I'll leave the presidency more idealistic": Bill Clinton, Farewell Address, January 18, 2001.

90 As he left the White House, his approval: "Presidential Approval Ratings—Gallup Historical Statistics and Trends," Gallup.

90 "There are no final victories in politics": Bill Clinton, Civil Rights Summit, LBJ Presidential Library, April 9, 2014.

91 "he could speak almost fondly": Taylor Branch, *The Clinton Diaries*, 8.

91 Hillary often joked that he forgot: Bill Clinton, Good Trouble Gala, John Lewis Foundation, Washington, DC, June 3, 2024.

92 He showed Clinton the quarry: David Smith, "Nelson Mandela's Cell Neglected and Unvisited, 50 Years After Rivonia Speech," *Guardian*, April 18, 2014.

92   "Yes," Mandela replied: Clinton, *My Life*, 417–18.

93   "It's my job to do it": Jose Del Real, "Clinton Recalls Lessons from Mandela," *Politico*, December 8, 2013.

93   "I did not even remember what happened": Ibid.

GEORGE W. BUSH / GIVING BACK

96   "an inflection point": Interview with the author for Updegrove, *The Last Republicans*.

96   "a priority": Ibid.

96   "lived a little too large": Ibid.

96   "a better man": Ibid.

97   "There was no lecture, no grabbing of the shoulders": Ibid.

97   As Bush conceded later: George W. Bush, *Decision Points*, 34.

97   "timeless truth": George W. Bush, Speech on US International Development Agenda, Washington, DC, May 31, 2007.

98   "To whom much is given, much is required": Ibid.

99   "some sort of expectation": Interview with the author for Updegrove, *The Last Republicans*.

99   "bloom" where he was "planted": Gary L. Gregg II, "George W. Bush: Life Before the Presidency," Miller Center, Millercenter.org.

100 "complementary souls": Laura Bush, Interview with the author, Texas Book Festival, October 16, 2010.

100 "My biggest liability in Texas": Eric Pooley with S. C. Gwynne, *Time*, June 14, 1999.

101 "war president": "George W. Bush: The 9/11 Interview," *National Geographic*, August 2011.

101 In the mournful and uncertain days: "Presidential Approval Ratings—George W. Bush," Gallup.

102 "The face of terror is not the true faith": Robin Wright, "Presidents Obama, Bush Sound a Lot Alike on Countering Islamic Extremism," *Wall Street Journal*, February 19, 2015.

102 AIDS had killed more than twenty million: George W.

Bush, Remarks on Signing the US Leadership Against HIV/ AIDS, Tuberculosis, and Malaria Act of 2003, Washington, DC, May 27, 2003.

102 Seventy percent of those afflicted: Laura Bush, *Spoken from the Heart*, 329.

102 "Less than two percent": Michael Gerson, "George W. Bush's Words in State of the Union Saved Millions of People," *Washington Post*, February 11, 2013.

103 "solve Africa's problems": Sheryl Gay Stolberg, "In Global Battle on AIDS, Bush Creates Legacy," *New York Times*, January 5, 2008.

103 "If you believe that America": Interview with the author, "Bush 2.0," *Texas Monthly*, December 2010.

103 "My thinking was significantly affected by 9/11": Ibid.

103 Fauci's recommendation: Stolberg, "In Global Battle on AIDS."

104 "wanted to do something game-changing": Ibid.

105 Twice during his presidency: George W. Bush, *Decision Points*, 351.

108 In August 2005, Hurricane Katrina: Kim Tyrrell, Kristen Hidreth, and Shelly Oren, "The Storm That Changed Disaster Policy Forever," National Conference of State Legislatures, April 14, 2022.

108 "uniter not a divider": Rich Lowry, "I'm a Uniter, Not a Divider," *Washington Post*, October 8, 2000.

108 "I have followed my conscience": George W. Bush, Farewell Address, Washington, DC, January 15, 2009.

108 By the time he had left office: George W. Bush, *Decision Points*, 353.

109 "I don't know, but I know I won't be around": Interview with the author for Updegrove, *The Last Republicans*.

110 On the other, the costly wars: Daniel Brown and Azmi Haroun, "The Wars in Iraq and Afghanistan Have Killed at Least 500,000 People, According to a Report," Military.com, August 29, 2022.

110   Still in effect, the program: Nicholas Kristof, "When George W. Bush Was a Hero," *New York Times*, April 8, 2023.

110   "You may recall that I spent eight years": Ibid.

BARACK OBAMA / GRACE

112   "Is your hair like mine": "President Obama Reunites with the Young Man from One of His Favorite Photos," Obama Foundation, Obama.org.

113   "knowing what that little gesture meant": Interview with the author and Mark Lawrence, *With the Bark Off* podcast, October 7, 2022.

113   "kids all around this country": Barack Obama, *A Promised Land*, 77.

113   "The presidency has made": Jenna Johnson and Karen Tumulty, "Trump Is Changing the Presidency More than the Presidency Is Changing Trump," *Washington Post*, February 9, 2017.

117   "I was engaged in a fitful interior struggle": Barack Obama, *Dreams from My Father*, 77.

117   That included him: Ibid., 82.

117   "utterly alone": Ibid., 91.

117   "dabbled": Michael Nelson, "Barack Obama: Life Before the Presidency," Miller Center, Millercenter.org.

118   "we have a stake in one another": Barack Obama, *The Audacity of Hope*, 2.

121   At a victory celebration: *Vanity Fair*, November 5, 2008.

121   That feeling of manifest pride, even elation: "Presidential Inauguration Draws 20.6 Million Viewers," Nielsen, January 2013.

121   "We know everything we do or say": Peter Baker, *Obama*, 128.

122   It was the kind of demeaning situation: Barack Obama, *A Promised Land*, 395.

122   "acted stupidly": Ibid., 396.

122   "he was going to be different": David Simas, interview with the author.

123   "That makes sense to me": Ibid.

123   "shock absorber": Ibid.

123   "With all that you have on your plate": Barack Obama, *A Promised Land*, 398.

124   "I'm good": Ibid., 537.

124   "useless, without purpose": Ibid., 538.

125   "heart bigger": Ibid., 539.

125   "The work, I loved": Ibid.

125   "The deepest fault lines of our democracy": Gardiner Harris and Mark Landler, "Obama Tells Mourning Dallas, 'We Are Not as Divided as We Seem,'" *New York Times*, July 11, 2016.

127   "I always tell young people": Bill Chappell, "'We Are Not Cured': Obama Discusses Racism in America with Marc Maron," NPR, June 22, 2015.

127   "one isn't confined to one's dreams": Barack Obama, *The Audacity of Hope*, 241–42.

128   "humbling": Barack Obama, Civil Rights Summit, LBJ Presidential Library, April 10, 2014.

128   "You're reminded in this great democracy": Ibid.

BIBLIOGRAPHY

Baker, Peter. *Days of Fire: Bush and Cheney in the White House.* New York: Doubleday, 2013.

———. *Obama: The Call of History.* New York: New York Times, 2019.

Becker, Jean. *The Man I Knew: The Amazing Story of George H. W. Bush's Post-Presidency.* New York: Twelve, 2021.

Bourne, Peter G. *Jimmy Carter.* New York: Scribner, 1997.

Branch, Taylor. *The Clinton Diaries: Wrestling History with the President.* New York: Simon & Schuster, 2009.

Bush, Barbara. *Barbara Bush: A Memoir.* New York: Scribner, 1994.

Bush, George. *All the Best: My Life in Letters and Other Writings.* New York: Scribner, 1999.

Bush, George, and Brent Scowcroft. *A World Transformed,* New York: Knopf, 1998.

Bush, George W. *Decision Points.* New York: Crown, 2010.

———. *41: A Portrait of My Father.* New York: Crown, 2014.

Bush, Laura. *Spoken from the Heart.* New York: Scribner, 2010.

Carter, Jimmy. *An Hour Before Daylight.* New York: Simon & Schuster, 2001.

———. *Keeping the Faith: Memoirs of a President.* New York: Bantam, 1982.

Carter, Jimmy, and Rosalynn Carter. *Everything to Gain.* New York: Random House, 1987.

Carter, Rosalynn. *First Lady from Plains.* New York: Houghton Mifflin, 1984.

Clinton, Bill. *My Life.* New York: Knopf, 2004.

Ford, Gerald. *A Time to Heal: The Autobiography of Gerald R. Ford.* New York: Harper & Row, 1979.

Klein, Joe. *The Natural: The Misunderstanding of President Bill Clinton.* 2002.

BIBLIOGRAPHY

Maraniss, David. *First in His Class*. New York: Simon & Schuster, 1995.

Meacham, Jon. *Destiny and Power: The American Odyssey of George Herbert Walker Bush*. New York: Random House, 2015.

Morris, Edmund. *Dutch: A Memoir of Ronald Reagan*. New York: Random House, 1999.

Morris, Sylvia Jukes. *The Price of Fame: The Honorable Clare Boothe Luce*. New York: Random House, 2014.

Obama, Barack. *The Audacity of Hope*. New York: Crown, 2006.

———. *Dreams from My Father*. New York: Times Books, 1995.

———. *A Promised Land*. New York: Crown, 2020.

Obama, Michelle. *Becoming*. New York: Crown, 2018.

Reagan, Nancy. *My Turn: The Memoirs of Nancy Reagan*. New York: Random House, 1989.

Reagan, Ronald. *An American Life*. New York: Simon & Schuster, 1990.

Smith, Jean Edward. *Bush*. New York: Random House, 2016.

Smith, Richard Norton. *An Ordinary Man: The Surprising Life and Historic Presidency of Gerald R. Ford*. New York: Harper, 2023.

Updegrove, Mark. *The Last Republicans: Inside the Extraordinary Relationship Between George H. W. Bush and George W. Bush*. New York: HarperCollins, 2017.

Updegrove, Mark. *Second Acts: Presidential Lives and Legacies After the White House*. Guilford, CT: Lyons Press, 2006.

Werth, Barry. *31 Days: The Crisis That Gave Us the Government We Have Today*. New York: Nan A. Talese, 2006.

Wright, Lawrence. *Thirteen Days in September*. New York: Knopf, 2014.

Yergin, Daniel, and Joseph Stanislaw. *Commanding Heights: The Battle Between the Government and the Marketplace That's Remaking the Modern World*. New York: Simon & Schuster, 1999.

ABOUT THE AUTHOR

Mark K. Updegrove is the author of four books on the presidency, including *Indomitable Will: LBJ in the Presidency*. The inaugural CEO of the National Medal of Honor Museum and the former director of the LBJ Presidential Library, Updegrove is a contributor to ABC News and *Good Morning America* and has written for the *Daily Beast*, *National Geographic*, the *New York Times*, *Parade*, *Politico*, *Texas Monthly*, and *Time*. He lives in Austin, Texas.